May the joy and peace of the Promises be yours, One Day at a Time!

CLEAR VISION PRESS

DENVER

Copyright © 2011 by Clear Vision Press

All rights reserved. No part of this book may be reproduced or transmitted in any form or by any means, electronic or mechanical, including photocopying, recording, or by an information storage and retrieval system, without express written permission from the publisher.

This publication is designed to educate and inspire—it is not meant to replace the advice of any mental health professional or recovery program. The author and publisher specifically disclaim any liability resulting from the use or application of the information contained in this book.

Clear Vision Press
2382 Norfolk St., Erie, CO 80516
(720) 375-2284
info@livingthepromises.com

www.livingthepromises.com

Printed in Canada

Publisher's Cataloging-In-Publication
    Madson, Jenifer
        Living The Promises: Coming to Life on the Road to Recovery
        Jenifer Madson.—1st ed.—Erie, CO : Clear Vision Press, 2011 p. ; cm

    ISBN: 978-0-9777770-6-8
        1. Self-help—Recovery Programs
        2. Self-help—12-Step Programs
        3. Self-help—Substance Abuse and Addictions
        I. Title

Design: Melanie Warner, Hotiron Creative, New York, New York
Editors: Barrie Hoople, Kristen Eckstein, Imagine! Studios, LLC

Living the PROMISES

coming to life

on the road

to recovery

dedication

To all who still suffer from addiction,
in and out of the rooms: may you find
a God of your understanding; may you
find recovery; may you find peace.

the a.a. promises

"If we are painstaking about this phase of our development, we will be amazed before we are half way through. We are going to know a new freedom and a new happiness. We will not regret the past nor wish to shut the door on it. We will comprehend the word serenity and we will know peace. No matter how far down the scale we have gone, we will see how our experience can benefit others. That feeling of uselessness and self-pity will disappear. We will lose interest in selfish things and gain interest in our fellows. Self-seeking will slip away. Our whole attitude and outlook upon life will change. Fear of people and of economic insecurity will leave us. We will intuitively know how to handle situations which used to baffle us. We will suddenly realize that God is doing for us what we could not do for ourselves.

"Are these extravagant promises? We think not. They are being fulfilled among us—sometimes quickly, sometimes slowly. They will always materialize if we work for them."

Alcoholics Anonymous: The Story of How Many Thousands of Men and Women Have Recovered from Alcoholism, 3rd ed. (Alcoholics Anonymous World Services, 1976)

This book would not have come to life without the support of countless people who encouraged me along the way.

acknowled

To my fellow "travelers": you led me to a Higher Power, which brought me grace; you welcomed me into the fellowship with open arms, which brought me love; you walked me through these magical steps—again and again—which brought me life. Words cannot express my gratitude; none of this is possible without you.

To author Karen Casey, who provided advice and encouragement from the moment the thought of this book arose: thank you for inspiring me since the very early days of my recovery with the love and hope that shines through you and your writing.

To Debbie Phillips, my masterful and loving coach: thank you for only ever seeing what is beautiful and possible for me by following my heart's calling.

To Ann Vertel, truly the best friend a girl could have: thank you for always telling me the truth, for keeping me focused on the future, and for being so full of integrity, spirit, and purpose.

Acknowledgments

To Melanie Warner, my wonderful friend and book designer:
thank you for bringing your creative genius to bear in
such an extraordinary way. Your patience and dedication
to this project is appreciated more than I can tell you.

To my family: thank you for loving me through the many
trials of my active addiction, and for supporting every
second of my recovery. Our ever-growing relationships are
a bigger gift of sobriety than I could ever have imagined.

To the Facebook and Twitter communities for *Living The Promises*:
thank you for inspiring me every day with your courage, determination, and love. Special thanks to Dawn B., Merle W., Roy N., Tom
R., Nancy J., Pam R., Stephen C., Joe O. and Barb P. for checking in
on me, pushing me forward, and giving me such valuable feedback.

And to my darling husband, Les: thank you for being you.
You are the warmest, kindest, most generous man in the
world; you hold my dreams as though they were your own,
and I am the luckiest woman alive to have your love.

When I got sober, just shy of my 24th birthday, the last thing I felt was the freedom and happiness that the promises speak of.

From th

I was sick: not just physically sick from the amount of chemicals in my system, but soul sick, completely bereft of a sense of spirit or purpose beyond finding a way to meet the day's craving.

I remember very little about my first AA meeting besides crying and shaking so hard I could barely hold on to the cup of really bad coffee I was given. I certainly couldn't fathom why the people who gave me that coffee and then helped me find a seat would have any interest whatsoever in caring for the wreck I had become.

But I let them lead me nonetheless, because I had reached the very bottom of my particular hell.

I wasn't a skid-row drunk. I was a middle-class, puke-every-morning-until-I-could-get-the-day's-first-drink-to-stay-down, off-to-the-races-for-the-day-and-night kind of drunk. I was quite a functional alcoholic actually, which confused and worried my family, friends, and employers all the more because they couldn't grasp how I could be so messed up and still show up for things—mostly on time and ready to do what was called for at any given moment.

That doesn't mean I was any good at anything. Quite the contrary, I was just good enough to give you a glimpse of some greater potential, just good enough to compel you to keep me around; just good enough to get by.

So nobody saw any need to intervene with me because I stayed one tenuous step ahead of any real consequences of my addictions. I mixed my chemicals in a way that kept me up when I needed to be up, down when I needed to come down, and completely wasted when that's what it took to keep up with the people I ran with. For years, I chose only the people, places, and professions that I could manipulate to support my addictions. In the end, I drank and drugged because I couldn't not drink or do drugs. I drank and used whether it was sunny or rainy, life was good or not so good, or because it was Tuesday. Or because it wasn't.

All along, deep inside me, I knew something was wrong, that how I interacted with alcohol and drugs wasn't right or good or normal. I just didn't know what to do about it.

In this book, I tell my story of recovery, as suggested by our 12-Step programs: I will tell you what it was like, what happened, and what it is like now, not with "drunkalogues" to convince you of my qualifications, but with stories and sayings and strategies that might help you or someone you know get sober, stay sober, and live a life of joy.

That is my life today. It's not a perfect one, but it is a joyous one, because no matter what is happening on any given day, I never lose sight of the amazing blessing of my sobriety; the incredible freedom it gives me to be who I want to be, to go where I want to go, and to serve others in ways I had never imagined. I know that reaching out in this way gives me yet another day of peace.

FOR THAT, AND FOR SO MUCH MORE, I AM GRATEFUL.

> "If we are painstaking about this phase of our development, we will be amazed before we are half way through."

introdu

This sentence leading into the 9th Step Promises opened my eyes to the fact that if I carefully and methodically did the preceding step work, I would see significant progress in my recovery in a very short time.

At the time I first read that passage, my downs dramatically outweighed my ups, and I was way more accustomed to being horrified and ashamed than to being amazed. So that was my first real sense of promise from the 12 Steps; that if I were thorough in my inventory, in humbly sharing that inventory, in making my amends, and in doing whatever was necessary to repair the damage of my past, I would start to experience a very important personal shift.

But I couldn't figure out what amazement would be like exactly—would it be a big, one-time, burning-bush moment? Or an ongoing, smell-every-rose, daily zest for life?

I didn't know how to answer those questions, I just knew that I desperately wanted to replace the sadness and uncertainty that I felt most days, and amazement sure sounded like a great alternative.

But before I could truly know any of the 9th Step Promises, amazement included, I first had to go through the eight preceding steps. The first step—admitting that I was powerless over alcohol and that my life had become unmanageable—was the easy one, one for which I had plenty of evidence. After all, it was the powerlessness

and unmanageability with alcohol and drugs that had led me to an AA meeting and put the Big Book into my hands to begin with.

The next seven steps gave me quite a bit more trouble, and it took me more than a year to work through them. But by the time I finished, I started to feel what I believed it meant to be amazed, which was this pervasive wonder from seeing my life evolve into something beautiful and useful.

My amazement—and usefulness—grew with each formal pass through the steps, which I did three times in the first five years of my sobriety. Along the way, my life turned from an unrelenting horror into this remarkable daily experience to look forward to.

And each subsequent time I have worked these steps, whether formally or informally, I have become more and more willing to be searching, fearless, moral, and honest, and my life and ability to serve others has improved proportionately.

WHICH IS AMAZING. STILL.

january

"We are going to know a new freedom and a new happiness."

JANUARY 1

When I first heard this promise, I couldn't remember the last time I had felt a happiness that wasn't chemically induced, much less one that originated from some deep, authentic place.

As for freedom, I was constantly on the run from my lies and manipulations, so if nothing else, I hoped that this meant that I could stop looking over my shoulder, could stop trying to remember what I had said or done, and could stop trying to cover my tracks all the time.

I had no idea that it would come to mean the ultimate freedom of being able to go wherever, to do whatever, and to be whomever I wanted. Even more, it came to mean that by doing things in service to others first, as best as I could on any given day, I would spend most days feeling like **I COULD ACHIEVE ABSOLUTELY ANYTHING I PUT MY MIND TO.**

JANUARY 2

> I am grateful for the freedom that comes from surrender. When I stopped fighting and started following, stopped talking and started listening, I started to heal.

People in early sobriety often pretend to have all the answers to this recovery deal and are quite willing to share them with anyone who will listen.

I was no different. Fortunately, I had old-timers—some not so patient in the process—who would sit me down and set me straight on the real deal: my ego and addiction were what had gotten me into this mess, and it was surrender and a God of my understanding that would get me out of it.

I JUST HAD TO LET GO.

JENIFER M

JANUARY 3

Sometimes a day is just a day. Maybe there doesn't need to be anything particularly profound in it except our sense of gratitude for having it.

We don't always need something big to happen to prove we're in the game. Sometimes, just calmly, patiently showing up is enough. No hoopla, no drama, no parade, just a day.

LET TODAY UNFOLD.

JANUARY 4

When it's all said and done, only love and service matter.

We spend a lot of time and energy on how we feel in sobriety, as though feeling good is the mark of success.

And while it's great to feel better when we clean up, the real victory is our growing ability to give: to give love, support, encouragement, or laughter—sometimes just to give a cup of coffee.

THE REAL MEASURE OF SUCCESS IS OUR GROWING CAPACITY TO CARE FOR OTHERS.

JENIFER M

JANUARY 5

Practice life with people, not on them.

Getting clean, sober, and clear directs us to be completely up front about our motives and to no longer use people for our own selfish gains.

We are released not only from our obsession with alcohol and drugs, but also the compulsive need to take people hostage.

DON'T JUST CHECK YOUR MOTIVES; REVEAL THEM.

JANUARY 6

Freedom begins when you choose humility over humiliation.

Many of us continue to humiliate ourselves in recovery by letting our pride stand in the way of admitting what we don't know and not following better instructions.

So we choose blindly, again and again, and create more things to be sorry for because we insist on going it alone, until finally, hopefully, we surrender and ask—humbly—for help.

The difference between humility and humiliation is simple: humiliation brings regret, humility brings relief.

CHOOSE RELIEF.

JANUARY 7

Do the next right thing, do it the right way, and do no harm in the process.

A great formula for deciphering "the next right thing" is first what will keep me sober, next, what will keep me sane, and finally, what will put me in service.

Doing it the right way means being as selfless as possible in the process.

DOING NO HARM MEANS HAVING THE RIGHT INTENTION TO BEGIN WITH, NOT TRYING TO CONTROL THE OUTCOME, AND TURNING THE RESULTS OVER TO MY HIGHER POWER.

Living the Promises

JANUARY 8

There is no surer way to relieve my own suffering than to help someone else relieve theirs.

First, get some perspective on your suffering: see if it's real or imagined or just a place where you've chosen to hide for a while.

Next, find true gratitude for your circumstances, no matter how painful they may be.

Finally, turn your attention to someone else, even if in a small way. Go to a meeting, take a newcomer to coffee, clean up the meeting room, or just be a good listener.

FOCUS FORWARD, TOWARD SOME GREATER GOOD, AND YOU'LL BE "OUT OF SELF" IN NO TIME.

JANUARY 9

It's a life full of possibility when I choose wonder over worry.

We go from being in a constant state of worry from lying, cheating, and stealing our way through life to facing our fears, taking inventory, asking for help, and making amends.

Clearing the wreckage of our past with such great scrutiny is what makes room for boundless wonder and curiosity, for infinite solutions and promise.

I KNOW NO GREATER PATH TO FREEDOM.

JANUARY 10

It's a great moment when you realize that your life has become something to enjoy rather than something to constantly repair.

Our fellowship gives us an environment in which to spread our wings, try new things, get to know people, and start to have some real fun again.

We no longer have to spend our time cleaning up another mess that we've made; we can finally show up for life and celebrate.

ENJOY THE DAY.

JENIFER M

JANUARY 11

"The good news is..."

...whatever you want it to be.

What an amazing new outlook, to be able to find some good in every situation, no matter how crazy or baffling it may be.

FIND THE GOOD NEWS.

Living the Promises

JANUARY 12

What if everyone did know their own strength?

Better yet, what if we not only knew it, but were all committed to using it for everyone's good?

It would be extraordinary to live in a world that was committed to combining our given talents for the good of all.

I CAN'T CONTROL HOW OR WHEN ANYONE ELSE DOES IT, BUT I CAN DO MY PART.

JANUARY 13

Look for signs of growth. Chances are, you won't have to look too far.

Let the little signs be as good as the big ones.

Don't wait for the big victories before you celebrate.

LOVE THE JOURNEY.

JANUARY 14

I am grateful for the freedom my recovery gives me to love and be loved.

I am grateful that I got my life back.

I am grateful for my spiritual awakening.

I am grateful that I can carry the message.

I AM GRATEFUL FOR ALL OF YOU.

JENIFER M

JANUARY 15

Me: "This is hard. I want to drink."

Sponsor: "Honestly, what good would that do?"

My sponsor was a woman of few words, was usually practical and neutral, but always warm and curious. She was intensely committed to AA, but never acted like she cared more about my sobriety than I was willing to. She taught me to never pursue a "distancer." She taught me to stop whining and start celebrating, to look inward only to improve my ability to help others, not to find fault with myself. She never assumed I knew how to do this sobriety thing, but also didn't chase me around to make sure I was making time for it. She had a normal, sometimes messy life, but never used it as an excuse not to be sober and of service.

She knew how to say "no" to me, and "yes" to my recovery.

AND BECAUSE OF THIS—AND SO MUCH MORE—I AM MORE VALUABLE TO THE WORLD.

JANUARY 16

Stop quibbling: Get out of "yeah, but…" and into "yes, and…".

We think we're so smart. And we are, but smart and wise aren't always the same.

Smart has all the answers.

Wise takes time to ask questions, consider the information, and make a careful choice.

LEARN TO DISCERN THE DIFFERENCE.

JANUARY 17

"The armchair is the spaceship for the insane. Get up, get out, and get into life already!" (Heard in a meeting)

Meetings are easy. Everyone loves that we're there and that we are sober and clean yet another day.

The hard part is getting into life, with all its messiness, and applying what we've learned in the rooms.

Fortunately, we've got the tools—the slogans, tips, books, people, steps, and Higher Power—not only to live life clean and sober, but to love it on its own terms.

LIVE IT UP.

JANUARY 18

We start to experience real progress on our path when we get more committed to asking the right questions than to having all the answers.

I learned early on that my life ran most smoothly when I stopped pretending to know things that I clearly didn't, started admitting what I didn't know, and asked for help in the process.

And I not only became more open to suggestion, I began to ask smarter questions.

I WENT FROM ASKING,
"WHY CAN'T I...", TO
"HOW CAN I...", TO
"HOW CAN I *BEST*..."

JANUARY 19

> I came to believe not only that a power greater than myself could restore me to sanity, but also that a purpose greater than I awaited my transformation.

It's easy to fall into the trap of thinking that our life's purpose has to be this massive, Mother Theresa-like goal to save the whole world in order for it—or us—to matter.

It can be just as significant to do our part to improve the world wherever we go, whatever way we can.

FIND YOUR PURPOSE.

JANUARY 20

All right, who hid my excuses?

It didn't matter what I whined about, my sponsor had a solution, a better perspective.

And in meetings, it never seemed to fail: on the days I held myself back from any and all offers of help and had made up my mind that no one had anything to say that could help my terminally unique life, someone's comments would break through at the eleventh hour, and I would hear what I needed to have another sober day.

SHOW UP FOR YOUR SOLUTIONS.

JANUARY 21

Go from "I'll be happy when…"

to "I'll be happy, then…"

Then to "I'll be happy."

Then to

"I AM HAPPY."

JANUARY 22

It's not "my life" or "your life" that we contend with: it is simply life, with all its ups and downs.

Time in the program doesn't give anyone a lock on a better life.

The quality difference in someone's sobriety is in the grace, perspective, and humor with which they meet its endless uncertainties.

What time in the program gives you is the opportunity to repeatedly practice living this way until that becomes your "new normal."

PRACTICE WHAT YOU WANT YOUR LIFE TO BECOME.

JANUARY 23

"Walking your talk" is not just a suggested way of being in the program, it is a responsibility, your beacon to guide those still suffering to a better way of life.

We are service in action by our thoughts, words, and deeds. We are living proof that this 12-Step thing works.

LIVE YOUR PRINCIPLES.

JANUARY 24

Never lose sight of the opportunity sobriety gives you to forge a new identity.

No one is perfect—we all have bad days and act out in ways we're not too proud of.

Fortunately, the program teaches us how to conduct ourselves in a more reasonable manner; we no longer have to be known for being irrational, inappropriate, moody, or any of the other negative traits that characterized us when we were using.

WE CAN BECOME KNOWN FOR THE PEOPLE WE ARE BECOMING, NOT THE ONES WE ONCE WERE.

JANUARY 25

Learn to see things as they are, not better or worse than they are.

Don't react, respond: take the emotions out of the situation, and give rise to the innate wisdom that can move you in the most productive direction.

The emotions can be positive or negative; when we become overly consumed by either, we can lose sight of the best course of action.

CONSIDER YOUR OPTIONS, IN ANY GIVEN SITUATION, FROM A CALM, OBJECTIVE, MIDDLE GROUND.

JANUARY 26

The monk: "You are happy, always so happy. Why so?"
Me: "Why not?"

People used to just see me as "intense." And I was, but not in a good way, or for the right reason. I was not intense so much as I was just tense, as in wound up and afraid.

The steps "unwound" me and taught me to truly connect, and love, and trust, not to just barrel impatiently and fearfully through life.

Then people stopped saying "intense," and started saying "happy."

AND THE DAY I REALIZED THAT MY IDENTITY HAD SHIFTED IN THAT WAY WAS A HAPPY DAY.

JENIFER M

JANUARY 27

What I insist I don't need to work on is probably what I most do.

And the people we react to most negatively are probably the ones who most clearly reflect those characteristics, situations, or reactions that we need to improve in ourselves.

Rather than being annoyed at them for mirroring our defects, we can feel blessed for being shown—and having seen—what needs to change.

IT'S A GOOD DAY FOR PROGRESS.

Living the Promises

JANUARY 28

Raise your sights; raise your standards.

It's ok to improve our standard of living, whether in our relationships, careers, finances, or material possessions.

And raising the standard of our thoughts, our speech, and our actions is the first step to improving our circumstances.

IT'S NOT ABOUT BECOMING BETTER THAN ANYONE ELSE; IT'S ANOTHER WAY TO BECOME A BETTER YOU.

JANUARY 29

Sobriety gives me the ultimate freedom to do what I want, to go where I want, and to be whomever I want. I pray to use those gifts wisely, in service to others.

We get clean and sober and open the door to a brave new world, full of possibilities. The trick is to take advantage of these opportunities without becoming "self-will run riot," or doing things and going places that put us, others, or our sobriety in harm's way.

We must be vigilant in the world, but not afraid of it, because the whole point of getting clear of our addictions is to become "happy, joyous, and free."

WITH A CLEAR HEAD AND THE RIGHT MOTIVES, GO LIVE LIFE TO THE FULLEST.

Living the Promises

JANUARY 30

Such grace. I'm speechless.

Seeing grace at work in our recovery, usually in spite of the most ridiculously negative conditions, and watching us grow, mature, soften, and love creates not just happiness for me today, but pure, unadulterated joy.

— JENIFER M

Live.

JANUARY 31

Living the Promises

February

> "We will not regret the past nor wish to shut the door on it."

FEBRUARY 1

At what point did my sobriety go from being about the horror I was trying to get away from to the brilliant life I was moving toward?

It happened when I finally believed that I was worth saving, not just that you believed it. That came from showing up—again and again—to hear the same, predictable platitudes—again and again—about "one day at a time" and "this too shall pass" and "let go and let God," and a hundred others just like these. And you wouldn't stop talking about the progress in your life from following these directions, so I finally started listening.

After hearing came contemplation, and from contemplation came application and action. From that application came freedom, a bit at a time, then joy. By focusing on the similarities over the differences, **I FINALLY SAW THE GREAT HUMAN POTENTIAL THAT IS IN EACH OF US**, self included, not just in those who seemed more worthy of grace and opportunity.

Living the Promises

FEBRUARY 2

> Don't visit the past to second-guess yourself. Instead, create a "second-strategy": only look back to identify the change in thoughts, language, and action that can lead you to a better future.

Beating ourselves up over past mistakes does nothing but weaken us physically, mentally, emotionally, and spiritually. The beautiful blessing of this program is that it gives us the tools to redo anything we think we've failed to do up to this point in our lives, if we so choose.

If you insist on looking backward, only give yourself permission to do so if you are committed to growing from it or determining who else might be due some amends from it.

OTHERWISE, LET IT BE.

JENIFER M

FEBRUARY 3

I started to take a stand for my life when I learned to assert myself—once I kept "just," "kind of," and "maybe" from dominating my language, I stopped sounding like I was apologizing for my existence.

I can now be decisive without being a jerk about it.

I can now stand my ground without insisting that you stand with me.

I can now claim an opinion without insisting that you agree.

I AM SOBER, HEAR ME ROAR (calmly, yet assertively).

FEBRUARY

4

Live your vision, once you claim it.

It is fine to borrow other people's vision of a happy life until we can create our own; trying on other people's way of life is one way we begin to figure out what really matters to us.

The beauty is, the more we do the step work, the better we are at gauging how and where we individually want to shine, and the better we are at trusting our own opinions about that as much as those of others.

STOP DOUBTING AND START CREATING THE LIFE YOU DREAM OF—TIME AND EXPERIENCE WILL TEACH YOU HOW TO MOLD IT, DAY BY DAY.

FEBRUARY 5

Let people see more for you than you can see for yourself.

We are such wrecks when we hit the doors of recovery that sometimes it's hard for us or anyone else to see past the fatigue and shame to our beautiful potential.

But can you imagine life today without the people in the rooms who insisted there was more to us than what we walked in with? If it weren't for those folks, our many dreams and talents might be lost forever.

As it is, they may only be temporarily displaced.

REVISIT YOUR POTENTIAL.

FEBRUARY 6

Everyone has their own path in sobriety. Some never reach a better destination, some do. I am their fellow traveler, there to accompany them, not to condemn.

It's hard not to interfere or to judge harshly when we see someone going down a road that we think is sure to lead to heartache or trouble, but it's rarely up to us to manage people's choices or to divert them.

Sometimes the best we can do is to walk beside them, to not abandon them in their confusion.

Sometimes they just need a gentle nudge to get on a better path.

SOMETIMES THE SOFTEST SUGGESTION SPEAKS THE LOUDEST.

JENIFER M

FEBRUARY 7

If someone points out something about you that you don't like, don't get mad, get even; even-keeled, and willing to take away what's useful.

Receiving unpleasant information—taking it with a grain of salt, if you will—means being willing to take a little taste of it, to try a bit at a time before chewing on the whole message.

Be determined to be curious: to **"TAKE THE BEST, AND LEAVE THE REST,"** even—or especially—if the information is a little hard to swallow at first.

Living the Promises

FEBRUARY 8

Refining our speech—minimizing profanity, for instance—opens the door to asserting ourselves in much more productive ways.

Coarse speech can be a place to hide when we're feeling insecure—it sounds more confident than we often feel.

But if you're going to use it, think it through, and do so to make a useful point, or drop it.

THERE ARE SO MANY MORE EFFECTIVE WORDS ANYWAY.

FEBRUARY 9

> What is important is the degree to which we grow in sobriety, not how long we've been growing.

It's interesting to look back at what I struggled with in my early sobriety and what it's like for me now.

I worry less and wonder more. I am almost obsessive in my desire to learn new things and to share the fun of it with others. I want more to see people happy than to be right, and am more detached from others' insistence on being unhappy. I love my family more. I love my friends more. I say "I love you" more and I hug more.

REMEMBER, QUALITY OVER QUANTITY.

FEBRUARY 10

It's not enough that I don't intend to hurt or disrespect someone; I must rise to the level of managing my mind and conduct to ensure that I don't.

The inventory and amends process isn't there to be used as a crutch, or as a convenient broom with which to sweep up the mess I could have avoided if I had taken the time to be more thoughtful in the first place.

IT ONLY TAKES ONE EXTRA BEAT TO THINK BEFORE I SPEAK OR ACT.

FEBRUARY 11

If your intentions are good, if they are as pure as they can be, you may not always get things right, but at least you'll be in your right mind in the attempt.

To go from absolute selfishness to a vast concern for others is one of the bigger miracles of our sobriety. Most of us never thought we would care about anything but getting our fix.

Then we learned how to care about others for the right reason, which was simply because it was the right thing to do.

DO THE RIGHT THING UNTIL IT BECOMES THE BEST THING—THE ONLY THING—YOU KNOW HOW TO SET YOUR MIND TO.

FEBRUARY 12

Be willing to grow. Don't worry about whether you are more or less so than anyone else. Just be willing.

We addicts are a competitive lot. We no sooner stop puking and shaking and crying that we start comparing ourselves to others in the program; how long we've been here, which step we're on, what experience we had when we worked that step.

The problem is, our experience will never, ever be the same as someone else's. The good news is, our experience will be our own, with the help of many.

WILLINGNESS IS KEY.

FEBRUARY 13

The hardest, longest, and best day of my life was the day of my first meeting.

I wrestled mightily with the fear of the unknown as I waited for the meeting time to arrive, and then with the bigger fear, once I got there, that the beauty and hope of recovery was for everyone but me.

It took a while to realize that there was more than enough of both to go around.

I JUST HAD TO KEEP COMING BACK AND KEEP LETTING YOU LOVE ME THROUGH MY DAILY ANXIETY, UNTIL IT LESSENED, AND THEN EVENTUALLY WENT AWAY.

Living the Promises

FEBRUARY 14

Love is a verb.

DO SOMETHING LOVELY TODAY.

FEBRUARY 15

My sponsor: "Wherever you go, there you are. And wherever that is, you're always in the middle. Just make sure it's the best middle for you."

I didn't really understand that I had the ultimate choice in how I lived. Even though I had made the connection to how having too much to drink had led to me being a drunken mess, I couldn't figure out how to be on pace for a better future in every other aspect of my life.

And I was constantly comparing my insides to your outsides until my sponsor helped me see that trying to compete with everyone all the time was a waste of time: someone was always going to have more money than me, someone would always have less, someone would always be prettier, someone would always be less so, and so on. My job, she said, was to find what I wanted to be, or make, or look like, etc.—all on my own, for myself.

We stay sober, and we get to recreate our whole lives for the better, in whatever way we choose.

THAT'S CAUSE FOR CELEBRATION.

FEBRUARY 16

Stand tall, literally drawing yourself up straight and proud. At the same time, smile—and greet the day with quiet certainty.

You claim your rightful place in this world by getting clean and sober and becoming a contributing member of society. No matter what has gone before, if you are doing the work today of being in recovery and of service, then you have everything to be proud of.

SO SMILE, YOU'VE EARNED IT.

FEBRUARY 17

Be still. Stop talking, moving, thinking, judging, projecting.

You can gear up again later, but for now, settle down—if only for a moment—and rest.

DON'T WORRY; THE WORLD WILL BE WAITING WHEN YOU GET ON THE MOVE AGAIN.

FEBRUARY 18

Show up strong, give it everything you've got, and leave 'em wanting more!

If we are always lamenting Monday and celebrating Friday then we are seriously restricting our brilliance.

If I want more out of life, my job, and my relationships, then I'd better give it all I've got, every day of the week, because life will reward me in direct proportion to how strongly I show up for it.

BEST EFFORT DOESN'T ALWAYS LEAD TO BEST RESULT, BUT IT'S ALWAYS OUR BEST SHOT AT IT.

FEBRUARY 19

When faced with difficult situations, I can either apply graceful acceptance or irritable resignation. Only one leaves room for hope and action; I pray to choose wisely.

There is a significant difference between acceptance and resignation: the former leaves you receptive to what you can manage in the face of it, the latter with a sense of defeat.

Graceful acceptance of the situation doesn't mean I have to like it or even particularly be in action around it right away. It simply means I can rise above the need to rage against it.

GIVE RISE TO ACCEPTANCE.

FEBRUARY 20

In the beginning, "more will be revealed" meant more of the same ego-driven behavior I came in with. As I learned to surrender, and kept doing a searching, fearless, and moral inventory of my life, it came to mean more of my innate goodness and love.

We spend a lot of time in our beginning step work focused on what went wrong, maybe even avoiding our inventory because we're afraid to look at the wreckage of our past.

But the beautiful, delicate lotus flower arises from the dirtiest and thickest of mud, and so it is with our own value: as we push through the dirt that surrounds us, we radiate more and more kindness, integrity, reliability, humor, and compassion.

KEEP PUSHING.

JENIFER M

FEBRUARY 21

Instead of jumping to conclusions, imagine strolling up to them, reflecting on things you notice along the way. It might just give you the time you need to reach better ones.

Careful, thoughtful consideration; weighing your options; leaving room to be wrong; seeing things from all sides; suspending judgment; holding your tongue; investigating, then deciding. These are all marks of a very reasonable thinker.

Imagine that you have all the time in the world to engage these skills before making a decision and taking action.

IMAGINE.

Living the Promises

FEBRUARY 22

You're thinking anyway, you might as well think big.

"Big" as in your definition of big, not anyone else's.

Expanding your vision takes not only foresight, but also hindsight. You have to be able to sift through the past to find evidence of positive change to keep you motivated to keep reaching forward.

And then there's the tricky subject of whether you feel you're "worthy" of big.

IF NOT YOU, THEN WHO?

FEBRUARY 23

Unstuck is a beautiful thing.

I used to be nothing but stuck. Stuck in my delusions, stuck in the past, stuck up the creek without the proverbial paddle.

Unstuck happens by loosening my grip on what I've become attached to, whether that's a particular outcome, or reward, or a perception of what I may gain or lose.

I don't get stuck too much today if I remember that, no matter what, I can stay sober. As long as I've got that, I've got everything I need.

BEAUTIFUL.

FEBRUARY 24

The great thing about swiftly "cleaning your side of the street" is that it allows you to get on with the business of being of greater and greater service.

Check in: are there things you've said or done that have created unresolved situations that prevent you from moving on and being most useful or that you need to make amends for?

If so, deal with them, promptly.

YOU'LL BE SO GLAD YOU DID.

FEBRUARY 25

> Look to greet some part of every day with the curiosity of a child, free of preconceived notions. You'll be amazed at the new perspectives that become available to you.

The good news is, we don't have to rush to change our minds about everything all at once: we can suspend bits of our world views if we want.

Try to meet some part of the day with a completely open mind, as though it's the first time you've seen something or someone, and notice what that does to open everyone's minds a little.

IT MIGHT EVEN OPEN EVERYONE UP A LOT.

FEBRUARY 26

I may have to accept difficult things as they are in the moment, but that doesn't mean I have to get stuck there.

Our serenity prayer guides us to accept what we can't change and urges us to find the courage to change what we can.

And there is no set period of being in acceptance before I can move into change.

ACCEPTANCE AND COURAGE ARE NOT MUTUALLY EXCLUSIVE; EACH TAKES THE OTHER TO ACHIEVE.

FEBRUARY 27

In our rush to judgments, we often miss the opportunity to learn the most from the very people, places, and things we've just dismissed.

Lessons take many forms and come from countless, often surprising, sometimes maddening, sources.

Learn to be still and receptive, even (or especially) when the teacher is the most aggravating or arrogant.

EMBRACE THE MESSENGER.

FEBRUARY 28

Love.

FEBRUARY 29

It's your turn, dear reader. What is your thought for the day?

Living the Promises

JENIFER M

march

"We will comprehend the word serenity and we will know peace."

MARCH 1

For so much of my life—drunk and newly sober—I felt like I was crawling out of my skin, my nerve endings all jangly and exposed, constantly fueled by worry and restlessness.

And then I learned to breathe, and to pray, and I found peace and serenity in contemplation and meditation and in acting from compassion.

Serenity today comes from knowing that **I AM ENOUGH, IN THE EYES OF WHATEVER GOD IS, AND WORTHY OF PEACE AND PROGRESS, ONE DAY AT A TIME.**

MARCH 2

The only thing bigger than fear is faith. Focus on what you have deep, abiding faith in, and your fear will subside.

Have faith that you can stay clean and sober, by working the steps, just for today.

Have faith in the promises you can find evidence for.

Have faith in the ones you can't.

Have faith in whatever power is so much greater than you that you are able to feel hope in spite of yourself.

Keep cultivating that faith because the stronger it gets, the less room there is for fear.

HAVE FAITH THAT I—AND A MILLION OTHER RECOVERING ALCOHOLICS AND ADDICTS THAT YOU'VE YET TO MEET—BELIEVE IN YOU.

MARCH 3

Show up for life in a way that improves everyone's chances for success.

Don't leave the heavy lifting—of spirits, minds, intentions, or the meeting book—to everyone else.

TAKE THE LEAD IN CULTIVATING THE BEST POSSIBLE ENVIRONMENT FOR EVERYONE'S GROWTH.

MARCH 4

It takes what it takes—no more, no less—for each soul to surrender.

This is the hard truth that no one wants to hear when they ask how bad things must get for an active alcoholic or addict to get sober, stay sober, and live a productive life.

We don't have to have new answers for old problems. Keep it simple:

DIRECT THOSE STILL SUFFERING TO WHAT WORKS, AND LEAVE THE REST UP TO YOUR HIGHER POWER—AND THEIRS.

JENIFER M

MARCH 5

> "This too shall pass" is not just a slogan to help us through the hard times; it is a reminder of the impermanence of all things, a step to letting go.

I used to use this phrase to ignore what was happening, to hold my breath while I waited for things to change. I couldn't look at a difficult situation without reacting, so I would just close my eyes to it until some happier emotion or time could replace it.

I found out that happy times pass too.

I FINALLY REALIZED THAT LIVING FULLY MEANT LEARNING TO OPEN MY EYES AND BREATHE THROUGH WHATEVER WAS GOING ON, UP OR DOWN, HAPPY OR SAD. IT WAS HOW I CAME TO SEE AND TRULY APPRECIATE THINGS IN THE MOMENT.

MARCH 6

> The problem with claiming to be a perfectionist is that perfection is unachievable, so the claim and the pursuit create undue stress. Instead, simply enjoy the opportunity in sobriety to live a life directed by well-defined values and standards.

Perfectionism is just that: an ism, just like the rest of the ones we battle with. It is an affliction of the mind that causes us to be obsessed with getting what we want, often without regard to whether we are being beneficial in the process.

INSTEAD OF STRIVING FOR PERFECTION, FOCUS ON EFFECTIVENESS.

MARCH 7

The quality of our life depends, in part, on the degree to which we gracefully meet its tragedies and triumphs.

I had a ridiculous time, for quite a long time, managing my moods, and not just in the face of adversity.

Wild swings and expressions of thought and emotion ruled most of my days.

Righteous indignation was a common theme.

Forget compassion: I was too busy pitying you for missing the boat to share any empathy for our common condition.

I was either overly inflated or deflated, never buoyantly in the middle.

It was wearing me out and threatening my sobriety.

There was no easy answer. I just got sick and tired of being sick and tired and erratic in sobriety, so I worked on being less like that, and more like the happy, joyous, and free people.

OVER TIME, HAPPY, JOYOUS, AND FREE WON OUT.

Living the Promises

MARCH 8

Don't get so focused on the character defects of others that you lose sight of your own and miss the opportunity for them to be removed.

Don't deflect. Stay centered and focused on your own stuff, and don't let the temporary "pleasure" of finding fault in others take you away from working on your own.

YOU CAN'T DO THEIR WORK FOR THEM ANYWAY, SO YOU MIGHT AS WELL CONCENTRATE ON DOING YOURS.

MARCH 9

"Attraction rather than promotion" only happens if we carry ourselves with humble certainty, not certain arrogance.

There is nothing wrong with conviction, but people will only know by our works whether we are truly convinced of our path.

We just have to watch that our stance about the wonders of our recovery program doesn't become piteous or preachy.

WE DON'T HAVE TO SHOUT ABOUT THESE WONDERS; WE CAN SIMPLY BE A SHINING EXAMPLE OF THEM.

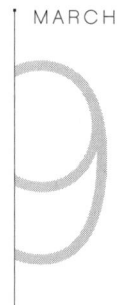

Living the Promises

MARCH 10

Be careful what you make of things without evidence to support your conclusion.

MARCH 11

Celebrate the little victories that come with being clean and sober.

Getting out of bed.

Making the bed.

Cleaning up after yourself.

Opening the drapes.

Opening the mail.

Returning phone calls.

Keeping food in the refrigerator.

Balancing a checkbook.

Paying the bills.

Paying the bills on time.

Showing up for work.

Showing up for work on time.

**BEING GRATEFUL.
(ACTUALLY, THAT'S A BIG ONE.)**

MARCH 12

Time in the program is a mark of survival, not necessarily of wisdom.

I was very focused on time in the beginning. If you had some, then you must know something I didn't.

Consequently, I fell in with and took bad advice from some folks early on who weren't drinking, but weren't exactly happy, joyous, and free either.

Fortunately, at the insistence of my sponsor, I started paying attention in meetings to whether people were walking their talk.

EVENTUALLY, I LEARNED WHAT IT MEANT TO "TAKE THE BEST, AND LEAVE THE REST."

JENIFER M

MARCH 13

People put their lives in our hands each time they give us their challenges in sobriety.

No one did me any favors by commiserating with me; it often made things worse by validating my wrong thinking and action.

Thank goodness there were people who were committed to leading me away from my problems by pointing me in the direction of my solutions.

THANK GOODNESS THEY WERE WILLING TO INCONVENIENCE ME IN THE MIDST OF MY WOES, FOR MY OWN GOOD.

Living the Promises

MARCH 14

Today I will soften—my stance, my judgment, my attitude.

We know that what is simple isn't always easy, and vice versa.

However, sometimes life is both.

HALLELUJAH.

MARCH 15

Sponsor: "You're not responsible for what pops into your head; you're responsible for what you do with it."

FORTUNATELY, OVER TIME, BOTH HAVE IMPROVED.

MARCH 16

Claim serenity, peace.

I lived in such a fretful world in my addiction, that on the rare occasion that I had a good day, I felt too guilty to enjoy it lest I leave any of my drama-filled buddies behind in the process.

I did leave some people behind when I finally chose a sober, happier life. I didn't dismiss them or lose my love and compassion for them, but I did leave them behind.

IT'S OK TO MOVE ON.

JENIFER M

MARCH 17

No one will take a stronger stand for your sobriety than you.

You gave me a meeting schedule, you didn't drag me in the door.

You gave me the book and told me how to study it, you didn't force me to read it.

You showed me an example of happy, joyous, and free, you didn't force me to want it.

You were happy to see me at yet another meeting, but you didn't place my sobriety before your own.

You gave me a place to grow, you didn't demand a time frame for it.

I had to be ready, you couldn't make it take hold.

YOU GAVE ME THE BLESSINGS, I HAD TO PROTECT THEM.

MARCH 18

Ground yourself with the confidence that, no matter what the question, you either know the answer or know where to get it.

This is the blueprint for becoming a phenomenal resource for the success of others.

NOTHING EVER FELT SO GOOD.

MARCH 19

Instead of finding fault, today I will find compassion.

We really don't have to look far to see our collective humanity.

We do have to be willing to look.

And let's not forget the seemingly limitless tolerance that others have had for our faults.

PERHAPS WE OWE THAT SENSITIVITY TO OTHERS.

MARCH 20

For every excuse I make about why something can't be done, someone, somewhere is making it happen under the same or worse circumstances.

Knowing this, I'm left with deciding whether I really want what I say I want, and whether it is something I will go to the ends of the earth to accomplish in spite of any perceived obstacles.

If so, great.

IF NOT, THAT'S OK TOO.

MARCH 21

Live with integrity and honor. Be in alignment with the values you've always had, that may have been hibernating while you were up to other things.

Integrity in sobriety is being who I say I am, and doing what I say I will do.

Living with honor means practicing these principles in all my affairs, developing good character, ethics, and morals, and consequently being able to hold my head up, knowing I have done these things, this day, to the best of my ability.

IF I THINK ABOUT IT, THIS INTEGRITY THING IS NOT A COMPLETELY NEW EXPERIENCE—MAYBE IT'S JUST BEEN DORMANT FOR A WHILE.

Living the Promises

MARCH 22

Express yourself.

Dance, sing, write, paint, craft, build, sculpt, draw.

TODAY, GO PLAY, BECAUSE YOU CAN.

MARCH 23

> We don't always have to strive and push for greatness. Sometimes good (truly good, not the false "fine" we sometimes use) is good enough.

Besides surrendering to powerlessness over alcohol, the surrender to the truth of my existence—and learning how to express that—was the key to improving my choice in how to be at any given moment.

AND THEN I REALLY WAS FINE.

MARCH 24

The more responsibility I took for my life, the more I grew up, the less dysfunctional everyone else appeared.

We see the world through lenses clouded by our own experience, for better or for worse.

If we are being dysfunctional, all we tend to see is dysfunction.

MAYBE IT'S TIME FOR A NEW PAIR OF GLASSES.

JENIFER M

MARCH 25

Stop telling old stories.

We come into sobriety with some very old, very limiting stories about what we are capable of.

Notice how often you use the following lead-ins to describe yourself and whether what follows builds you up or tears you down:

"I always..."

"I never..."

"I am..."

Chances are we are way more competent than we give ourselves credit for.

IT'S A GOOD DAY TO WRITE A NEW STORY BASED ON A RECOGNITION OF YOUR SKILLS.

Living the Promises

MARCH 26

Clarity, discernment, and joy came from being honest, open-minded, and willing.

I had to break through the clutter of my old thoughts, become newly curious, and develop new habits of honesty, open-mindedness, and willingness.

Before, I was motivated to do that so I wouldn't get drunk and die.

TODAY I'M MOTIVATED TO DO IT TO LIVE.

JENIFER M

MARCH 27

Intensity doesn't always equal care.

Sometimes it's just our futile attempt at trying to control the uncontrollable.

MARCH 28

You'll know you're doing "the next right thing" by your willingness to help the greatest number of people in the process, even if you're not one of them.

I'm not talking about codependence, where you neglect yourself in the process of giving everyone else your time and attention.

I'm speaking of your willingness to do what's hard, but right, and to still do it even if you don't benefit.

BELIEVE IT OR NOT, THE RIGHT THING CAN BECOME THE POPULAR THING.

MARCH 29

No one is immune to relapse.

If we're truly living a day-at-a-time philosophy, it is imperative that we do whatever will keep us sober today.

LORD KNOWS WE'VE GOT PLENTY OF TOOLS FOR THAT.

MARCH 30

My Higher Power didn't get me sober for my comfort, but so I can serve.

We are here to help each other. The only way we can do that is if we are free to do so.

The only way we are free is if we are clean, sober, and clear.

The only way I know how to be that is to practice the principles of the 12 Steps in all of our affairs.

THE DAY IS FULL OF CHANCES TO PRACTICE.

JENIFER M

Lead.

MARCH 31

Living the Promises

april

"No matter how far down the scale we have gone, we will see how our experience can benefit others."

APRIL 1

> I was afraid I hadn't gone far down enough, that my story wasn't dramatic enough to qualify me to be a member of AA, much less enough to move you to some greater action in your sobriety.

What I learned is that any story of redemption, "no matter how far down the scale," when told from the heart with a sincere desire to help another, is powerful enough to move mountains.

YOU HAVE A STORY. GO AHEAD AND TELL IT, JUST AS IT IS, WITHOUT EMBELLISHMENT, FREE OF ANY CONCERN ABOUT WHETHER IT IS GOOD ENOUGH TO TELL.

APRIL 2

Someone called me "an open book" the other day. I keep working to make sure it is one worth reading.

I was so secretive in my addiction, and even in early sobriety, that I didn't know how to truthfully relate to anyone. I was constantly making up stories about where I had been, what I had done, and how I felt, and I told them over and over until I believed them myself.

Then I did the work in the program of deconstructing the falsehoods of my past, and I learned to tell the truth, without exaggeration, with a sincere desire to be helpful in the telling.

I also learned how to honestly express my feelings: I learned they are just something I experience, they are not who I am.

WHEN IT'S ALL SAID AND DONE, I HOPE THAT MY LIFE'S STORY WILL ACCURATELY CONVEY THE MIRACLE AND HOPE OF MY RECOVERY.

JENIFER M

APRIL 3

> We don't always have to work so hard to shape and direct the day. Instead, greet the day with curiosity, fully open to what it might bring.

My life in addiction was very routine: get up, get high, try to make it through the day without anyone getting in my way, black out, pass out, wake up, do it again.

What passed for fun were the people, places, and things I put in place to support that routine.

It was a chore. A sometimes boring, but mostly frightening chore.

I went to the other extreme in early sobriety, always having to make the day be a certain way.

And then I figured out that being open and curious and spontaneous was a pretty fun way to go through life.

IT'S NOT ALWAYS A WALK IN THE PARK, BUT IT'S NEVER DULL.

APRIL 4

Most of us have way more talent than we give ourselves credit for. Don't be afraid to bring those skills into the light.

Sobriety gives us the chance to nurture and express any of a million talents, for our own development, as well as the enjoyment of others.

DON'T BE SHY, SHOW US WHAT YOU'VE GOT.

JENIFER M

APRIL 5

Live in an "and" world.

How often do you find yourself in either/or, black/white, now/then, always/never land?

ALWAYS? REALLY?

Living the Promises

APRIL 6

Wisdom manifests—sometimes quickly, sometimes slowly—from repeatedly working with life on its own terms.

We really didn't want to meet life on its own terms, and then we found that we had to, because there really wasn't another way to, and over time we develop so many tools that now it's a pleasure and a privilege to.

IT ALSO BECOMES QUITE THE ADVENTURE.

APRIL 7

For some part of the day, find silence.

Turn off the TV, unplug from the phone and Internet, find a comfortable place to sit, and simply relax and breathe.

When we achieve a relaxed state physically, we can then relax our minds, and a relaxed mind is the ground from which clarity springs.

SOME TIME, EVEN FIVE MINUTES LIKE THIS, IS ALWAYS BETTER THAN NO TIME.

APRIL 8

We are given a second chance to be trustworthy, loyal, and honest.

WHAT A GIFT.

APRIL 9

When you're looking for real answers, not just temporary relief, sometimes only stillness will do.

This is the only way I know to fully tap into my intuition, that place inside where God—whatever God is—lives.

It's that place where I know the beauty and joy of this precious human birth, where I am reconciled with impermanence, where I understand and respect the notion of karma, and where I once again commit to bettering myself for the sake of helping others.

AND WHATEVER THE QUESTION, I AM THEN OPEN TO THE ANSWERS.

APRIL 10

One of the secrets to gracious, conscious living is to choose what is right for you without making others wrong in the process.

IT'S A "LIVE AND LET LIVE" WORLD.

APRIL 11

Sometimes all the inspiration we need is the promise of a new day, whatever it brings.

AND THE PEACE OF MIND THAT WHATEVER THAT IS, WE HAVE THE TOOLS TO MAKE SOMETHING USEFUL OF IT.

APRIL 12

You know grace is limitless, right?

Anyone and everyone in this program is worthy of grace, simply by virtue of their humanity and a sincere desire to live a meaningful life.

And on those days when you're feeling like there is only so much grace to go around, imagine the countless number of once hopeless addicts and alcoholics who are finding relief and redemption today in countless meetings around the world—visualize the untold miracles that are in those seats at this very instant, and then tap into the sense of love and mercy that makes that so.

It doesn't matter where you've come from, or what you've done, or how much you have or don't have—**THE BLESSINGS OF SOBRIETY ARE THERE FOR THE TAKING. YOU JUST HAVE TO WANT IT.**

JENIFER M

APRIL 13

What would life be like if you were always the first to extend compassion and understanding, to offer the "olive branch" of peace, and to give others the benefit of the doubt?

We need to discover what prevents us from doing this and remove those obstacles.

BECAUSE LIFE WOULD BE REMARKABLE IF WE DID SO.

APRIL 14

Confronting an issue and being confrontational are two distinctively different ways of taking something or someone on. Pause when agitated, and be mindful of when one or both—or neither—is warranted.

We don't confront uncomfortable people or situations because we don't like conflict.

We are convinced that conflict is synonymous with fighting.

But at its core, conflict basically means disagreement.

In which case, my options in the face of conflict become pretty simple: agree, or agree to disagree.

WITH THAT IN MIND, I AM LESS LIKELY TO AVOID CONFLICT, AND MORE LIKELY TO WANT TO RESOLVE IT.

APRIL 15

Me: "How will I know if I've done my 4th Step right?"

Sponsor: "Be searching, fearless, and moral. If not, what hasn't been searched will find you, and you'll get to take another run at it."

She couldn't have been more correct. I wasn't ready to look deeply into my past the first time through my 4th Step.

Or the second time.

The third time was a bit of a charm, because I was finally ready to rid myself of the guilt and remorse that was holding me back from realizing a better version of life.

And the beauty of it was, the more I brought my greatest shortcomings into the light, the less power they had over me, until they eventually lost most of their emotional charge.

THAT'S WHEN THEY BECAME A SOURCE OF VALUABLE INFORMATION INSTEAD OF SHAME.

APRIL 16

> Mindfulness is the ability to suspend one's ego in order to see how best to apply our mind and conduct for the greatest good.

More simply put, it is the ability to get out of ourselves and into service to others, with the faith and confidence that this is why we're here.

And suspending one's ego is a delicate, ongoing dance, not a one-time occurrence, which is why **BALANCING YOUR MIND, EMOTIONS, AND REACTIONS IS SUCH AN IMPORTANT SKILL TO DEVELOP.**

APRIL 17

Life becomes infinitely simpler when I focus more on having a positive influence on the outcome than I do on trying to control it.

We shift from obsessing over how we can dominate to concentrating on how we can help.

IT'S A REALLY BIG SHIFT.

APRIL 18

We don't need drama—to create it or perpetuate it—to prove we're alive.

Overreaction is taxing, commiseration isn't helpful, and gossip is useless.

DRAMA IS JUST ONE MORE WAY TO GET PEOPLE TO PAY ATTENTION TO ME, AND WHEN I LOSE MY NEED FOR THAT, THE DRAMA MAGICALLY STOPS FINDING ME.

APRIL 19

Tell the truth, when it's the truth, only to the person(s) who can do the most good with it.

It's one thing to seek outside counsel in how to deal with something before you go back to the source.

IT'S QUITE ANOTHER TO WEAR OUT YOUR SIDE OF THE STORY EVERYWHERE BUT THE SOURCE.

APRIL 20

For every excuse I had, you gave me alternatives until I was left with nothing but possibilities.

THANKS FOR NOT LETTING ME STAY IN MY STUFF.

JENIFER M

APRIL 21

Pause.

Breathe.

Pray.

Do the next right thing.

REPEAT.

APRIL 22

A funny thing happened on the way to my sobriety: I finally looked up from my misery and saw a life worth living.

Maybe we don't choose recovery for all the right reasons in the beginning.

As long as we stay for the right reasons, we get an awesome shot at the coolest life imaginable.

ONE DAY AT A TIME.

JENIFER M

APRIL 23

"You have to give it away to keep it," they told me, and then showed me that while I didn't think I had anything to give, even one more day without a drink or drug meant I could give hope.

APRIL 24

When you feel wronged, skip the righteous indignation and go straight to compassion and forgiveness.

It clears the way to extraordinary growth.

(AND IT'S NOT NEARLY AS TAXING AS A BUNCH OF SANCTIMONIOUS HUFFING AND PUFFING.)

APRIL 25

Who says anger has to last?

If:

I can look at it from a better angle,

I can express it without causing harm,

I can call it by a new name,

then it has a chance to be something other than anger.

ALL OF WHICH CAN HAPPEN IN A FLASH.

APRIL 26

If nothing happens in HP's world by mistake, what are the coincidences in your life trying to teach you?

It's another kind of inventory, to look back at the end of the day and **INTENTIONALLY FIND THE LESSONS IN SEEMINGLY RANDOM OCCURRENCES.**

APRIL 27

It's only fair to let people know whether you're truly looking for advice and are open to suggestion or if you simply want support for what you've already decided.

APRIL 28

Today I'm eager to identify and let go of my character defects and make room for my character strengths to flourish.

Eager isn't exactly the word we would use in the beginning; anxious is more like it.

But the more we work these steps, the more we experience the joy of finding our new and improved selves.

And I, for one, would prefer to explore my strengths than to be held back by my weaknesses.

I'M SURE YOU WOULD TOO.

APRIL 29

If I change my "always," "never," and "have-to" stories, I'll change my outcome.

APRIL 30

Choose Joy.

JENIFER M

may

"That feeling of uselessness and self-pity will disappear."

Living the Promises

MAY 1

> My feelings of uselessness and self-pity were not a reaction to a true absence of skill or talent, but the by-product of a simple unwillingness to be helpful.

I felt useless because, the truth is, in my addiction I was useless, and I wallowed in self-pity because no one would buy my crazy excuses for why.

When I stopped using and started facing up to the truth of what I had become and engaged in the new life that recovery offered, I discovered strengths I never knew I had, like empathy, humor, insight, and compassion.

I found these strengths by putting myself to work—for myself, for others, and for the goals that slowly, but surely had become important to me.

BY DILIGENTLY FIGHTING TO GET BETTER AND BE BETTER, I FINALLY GATHERED ENOUGH EVIDENCE TO KNOW, IN MY HEART OF HEARTS, THAT I WAS INDEED USEFUL, IN SO MANY WAYS.

Living the Promises

MAY 2

Getting something you need may be the goal in standing up for yourself, but the real victory is summoning the courage to stand in the first place.

Standing up for myself isn't about lashing out at people who oppose me.

It isn't about false bravado either.

It's about saying what's true for me and asking for what I need or want.

ASKING WON'T GUARANTEE THAT I WILL GET IT, BUT IT SURE FEELS GREAT TO BE MY OWN ADVOCATE.

MAY 3

We are only doing as well on any given day as the skill set we access: our own, or someone else's. Don't let pride stand in the way of asking for what you need.

Your answers are out there, somewhere.

WIDEN YOUR NET, BROADEN YOUR HORIZONS, GET OUT OF YOUR OWN WAY, AND GO FIND THEM.

MAY 4

Find some greater sense of purpose, and you will find a source of energy and determination you never knew you had.

As soon as I make life about more than just me, I feel boundless and uplifted: not just by helping you, but by helping you help someone else be helpful to another who in turn helps another...

...AND SO ON.

JENIFER M

MAY 5

Become familiar with, then acquainted with, then accustomed to the truth.

We get clean and sober and hear about the truth.

Then we get searching and fearless and find our truth.

If we keep doing the work of inventory, amends, and awakening, we develop a habit of seeing and telling the truth.

THAT'S THE TRUTH.

MAY

6

We are better at love, life, and leadership than we can sometimes see.

Just because some of our romantic relationships or professional ventures haven't worked out, doesn't mean we'll never be any good at them; it may simply mean we haven't developed the right skills for them yet.

What does it mean to be a great leader? What are the qualities of a great relationship? Identify, define, and then embody those qualities, and you will be so much more likely to attract the same.

AND WHILE YOU'RE AT IT, GIVE YOURSELF CREDIT FOR THE BITS YOU ALREADY DO REALLY WELL.

MAY 7

We make a difference when we step up to serve others, proof of which may be hard to see. People's shifts are usually subtle; it is an extra blessing if we can witness the profound.

Service work may be what you are called to do or what you are skilled to do;

EITHER WAY, JUST DO IT.

MAY 8

Knowledge isn't power without the contemplation, use, and experience of it.

IN THAT ORDER.

MAY 9

Work these steps, and what you know and what you live will align.

In the beginning, and maybe for a good little while, there is something of a disconnect between what we intellectually want our lives to be like and what we literally choose in favor of.

It takes time and patience to close that gap and to fully live your principles.

YOU'RE UP TO THE TASK; LOOK AT HOW FAR YOU'VE COME ALREADY.

MAY 10

> I knew my choices in sobriety were improving—especially with relationships—when I no longer had to work overtime to rationalize or explain them.

Whether it is a friendship, a business relationship, or a romantic relationship,

if I am in it because of how I can enhance that person's life,

if I am there because I want to be, not because I have to be,

if I am willing to meet someone more than half way, and not afraid to kindly request the same,

THEN I STAND A PRETTY GOOD SHOT AT DEVELOPING AND MAINTAINING IT.

JENIFER M

MAY 11

We are meant for more peace and prosperity than our current struggles may indicate.

We may be used to struggling, but that doesn't mean we're destined for it.

It may simply have become a habit, which is understandable, considering how much drama and crisis we created in our addiction.

You can become more used to peace and prosperity the same way; by insisting on it, looking for it, cultivating it.

IT'S A VERY PRACTICAL PATH TO A MORE TRANSCENDENT WAY OF BEING, NO DOUBT.

MAY 12

Ego says "I've got this, move over and let me show you." Humility says, "Tell me more, show me how to put this in action, I'm grateful for the opportunity."

There's really no point to having all the answers or always having to be the one in charge.

NO GOOD POINT, ANYWAY.

MAY 13

> Someone else having more doesn't automatically mean you will have less. That would presume a limit to abundance.

It's tough, sometimes, to believe that there is truly more than enough of everything to go around, particularly in light of all the scarcity of the world.

But scarcity isn't about a lack of resources; it's more about the misapplication of the ones we've got.

We must learn to get creative and strategic about connecting with the source of what we need.

CONNECTING WITH OUR HIGHER POWER IS A GREAT START.

MAY 14

Today I will be calm, I will let any worry or negative projection fall away, and I will engage peacefully with whatever the day brings.

AND WHAT A DELIGHTFUL DAY THIS WILL BE FOR ME AS A RESULT.

MAY 15

Sponsor: "You're doing really well these days."

Me: "But I'm not where I want to be yet."

Sponsor: "Jenifer, just say 'thank you.'"

WHILE I DON'T ALWAYS HAVE TO AGREE WITH SOMEONE'S OPINION OF ME, I DON'T HAVE TO DENY THEM THE HOPE THEY MAY FEEL BY SEEING SOMETHING IN ME THAT THEY LIKE.

MAY 16

The present is perfect in some way: I simply have to be still enough to see and appreciate how.

This is easy when things are going our way.

It's on those days when everything and everyone seems to be working against us when we must totally commit to finding the good news in our situation.

BREATHING IS RECOMMENDED.

MAY 17

Focus on the "musts" in your life, those people, places, things, and thoughts that are critical to reaching the best possible outcome.

If you laid out every possible item that you think it would take to reach your ultimate outcome in any particular area of your life, and then looked deeply into the list, you would find that there are about 20% of those items that will get you 80% of your results.

THESE ARE THE "MUSTS." FOCUS ON THOSE.

MAY 18

Before, I spared no one my particular brand of bs. Now, I try to spare no one my love and compassion.

It's really exhausting to constantly try to enroll people in nonsense that serves only me.

It's so much more energizing to be open, kind, and authentically interested in the welfare of others.

I'M SURE THERE ARE PEOPLE OUT THERE WHO COULD USE A LITTLE MORE OF THAT TODAY.

JENIFER M

MAY 19

I've heard it said that no one can make you feel a certain way without your permission…today I take full responsibility for that notion.

There comes a time when we stop saying "you made me feel…" because we finally see that how we react to any given situation is fully within our control.

Then we are clear to sort out which feelings are most appropriate to the circumstances.

THAT'S FREEDOM.

MAY 20

Top 10 Gifts of My Sobriety:

(in no particular order)

The ability to ask for help.
A God of my understanding.
Finding joy.
Learning to love.
Gaining clarity and insight.
The absence of shame.
My relationships with family and friends.
The freedom to explore my gifts.
Meeting life on life's terms.

YOU.

MAY 21

Sobriety gives us this extraordinary opportunity to be better, to feel better...

to do better.

IMAGINE THE GOOD YOU CAN DO WITH THAT TODAY.

MAY 22

At our core, we are lovely, valuable beings.

We've just covered that person up with a lot of junk in our addiction.

For a while, it feels like we'll never come up for air.

And the people who support our recovery will be there while we dig our way out.

But it is ultimately up to each of us to wade through and clean up any garbage that hides or dampens our true worth.

FORTUNATELY, THERE'S A STEP FOR THAT.

JENIFER M

MAY 23

Just because we're alcoholics and addicts doesn't mean we get a pass on having manners.

A SOBER JACKASS IS STILL AN ASS.

MAY 24

It's a beautiful day when "Don't drink, go to meetings, get a sponsor, work the steps" ceases to be negotiable.

THIS IS THE DAY WHEN "SIMPLE" AND "EASY" START TO COEXIST.

JENIFER M

MAY 25

Today be the unflappable one, the one with no buttons to be pushed.

You can, you know.

GIVE IT A TRY, JUST FOR TODAY.

MAY 26

Don't let what you think you know get in the way of what you can—and need—to learn.

We ask for help, and then as soon as someone gives us some answers, we talk about how much we already know, or why their suggestions won't work.

Probably makes them wonder why we asked in the first place.

TRY BEING A BIT MORE CURIOUS TODAY, IN THE SPIRIT OF POSSIBLY LEARNING THE ONE LITTLE THING THAT COULD MAKE THE BIGGEST DIFFERENCE OF ALL.

MAY 27

People come and go, but spirit is forever.

My connection with a Higher Power is my bedrock, the one thing I can count on more than any person, place, or thing. It is from that confidence that I can grow and be more useful to others.

For a long time, I got it backwards: I put the pressure on people to be my saving grace.

YOU CAN IMAGINE HOW THAT TURNED OUT.

MAY 28

Letting others come first doesn't mean you come last; it means you made room for more than one person to win.

The person you allow in front of you in line at the store or in traffic; the person you pass to in a meeting, rather than take the last two minutes for yourself; the person you put up for praise in lieu of tooting your own horn: these are just a few of the opportunities you have to let someone else come first.

I'M SURE YOU CAN THINK OF A BUNCH MORE.

MAY 29

You can't build a new life on old thoughts and habits.

One of the biggest challenges in working a program of recovery is breaking our old habits.

It is hard to let go of old patterns; they may be uncomfortable, but at least they are familiar, and we do love certainty.

But we can be methodical in replacing our old habits with new ones; it doesn't have to be an all-at-once event.

As long as we stay open to the potential benefit of doing things differently, we've got a shot at making the shift.

WILLINGNESS IS THE FIRST STEP.

MAY 30

Never underestimate the power of service. You may be someone's only hope.

You never know when someone will need to see your happy, smiling face to know that they can do this recovery thing.

Make yourself available—go to meetings, be a sponsor, take a leadership position in the organization, for the sake of who you can serve.

YOU WILL GET MORE FROM THAT THAN YOU CAN EVER POSSIBLY GIVE.

Pause.

MAY 31

Living the Promises

june

"We will lose interest in selfish things and gain interest in our fellows."

JUNE 1

In my addiction, I constantly compromised what few principles I had if it meant I would get what I wanted, even though I greatly hurt the people I exploited along the way.

I brought those loose moral standards into my recovery, and, for a very long time, continued to capitalize on the strengths and weaknesses of others for my own gain.

But that behavior soon became painfully inconsistent with the more altruistic person I was becoming by working the steps.

So I first tried to be less selfish so I wouldn't feel so at odds with myself, a motivation which was still about me, but it was a start.

But eventually, my desire to serve others more than myself became an integral part of my nature, the manifestation of a powerful and deepening connection with my Higher Power.

IT'S NO SURPRISE HOW MUCH I AM CARED FOR IN THE PROCESS.

JUNE 2

> Spirit, honesty, insight, integrity—these were with me all along, just trapped in the darkness I created, waiting to once again see the light.

I was actually a pretty nice person before I became addicted to alcohol and drugs.

I faked being a nice person while I was in my addiction.

I had great qualities, I just used them for evil.

TODAY, I USE THEM FOR GOOD.

JENIFER M

JUNE 3

Clear the decks of anything or anyone that stands in the way of a real shot at a new life. Those who want the best for you will support you.

Some will do the best they can to support you and be pretty clumsy in the attempt.

Some will oppose your choices altogether, maybe out of fear that they will have to examine their own shortcomings.

EITHER WAY, DON'T BE AFRAID TO KINDLY ASK PEOPLE TO EITHER LEAD YOU IN THIS NEW LIFE, FOLLOW YOU IN IT, OR GET OUT OF YOUR WAY WHILE YOU PURSUE IT.

JUNE 4

> Everything we learn can be as much for someone else's benefit as for our own if we cultivate it for that reason.

You never know when the best lesson you learned is just what the doctor ordered for someone else.

This is why it's crucial to share our experience, strength, and hope, in and out of meetings.

If you're reluctant or embarrassed to do so, don't do it for you, do it for the person who might need to hear it.

TAKE ONE FOR THE TEAM.

JUNE 5

It is never wrong to trust your intuition when it moves you to serve others.

IT DOESN'T GET MUCH SIMPLER THAN THAT.

Living the Promises

JUNE 6

My mind may race from time to time, but at least today it's on a better track.

There is an untold loss of energy that goes with chasing the fear, projection, and "what ifs" of my mind.

I THINK I'LL SAVE MY STRENGTH FOR BETTER PURSUITS.

JENIFER M

JUNE 7

Trusting the process requires a healthy balance of faith and proof: I rely on faith as I build my evidence.

It's hard to find proof of progress in this program sometimes unless you're right in the middle of where it presents itself.

The best way I know to gather more than enough evidence that it works—when my own experience isn't enough—is in meetings.

Go to a meeting and what do you see? People of all ages, all backgrounds, with all different circumstances but the same affliction of the mind, body, and spirit working these steps and getting their lives together.

So if I'm going to meetings and still having a crisis of faith, it isn't about whether the program works; it's about whether I believe it will work for me.

AND WHY WOULDN'T IT?

Living the Promises | 185

JUNE 8

> There is nothing more egotistical than the belief that I, with all of my special problems, am somehow outside of my Higher Power's reach.

I am special, and I have special problems from time to time, but they are not unique, except maybe to me in that moment.

And just because they are unique to me, doesn't mean I should insist that you treat me with kid gloves while I work through them.

Instead, please insist that I stop using my terminal uniqueness to make excuses and to separate myself from everyone.

THANK YOU IN ADVANCE FOR HELPING ME GET OVER MYSELF.

JENIFER M

JUNE 9

Sobriety is not for the faint of heart.

We have to want it more than anything we ever have before.

AND WHEN WE HAVE THAT MOMENT OF CLARITY AND TRUTH AND COMMITMENT, THE WHOLE WORLD, IN ALL ITS CRAZY BEAUTY, OPENS UP TO US.

JUNE 10

No one got clean and sober alone. There is no shame in humbly asking for and gratefully receiving whatever help you need to stay that way.

And there is no shortage of what form that help may take. It might be in a meeting, a meeting before the meeting, maybe a meeting after the meeting...

YOU GET MY DRIFT.

JENIFER M

JUNE 11

We don't always need to feel great to know that the steps are working.

IT DOES HELP TO FEEL LIKE WE'RE MAKING PROGRESS THOUGH, SO INVENTORY THAT.

Living the Promises

JUNE 12

Smile in the face of whichever insanity is trying to win the day.

The best way to improve my mental state is to change my physical state—to actually do the opposite of what I'm stuck in when I'm angry or frustrated.

For instance, if I'm scrunching my eyes, I open them wide and use my fingers to spread out the wrinkles in my forehead.

If I'm frowning, I will make myself smile.

If I'm sitting and turned inward, I will stand up and lift my heart.

If I'm pacing and muttering, I will sit still and be silent.

If I'm breathing in a shallow way, I will take deep breaths.

TRY EACH OF THOSE, ONE AFTER THE OTHER, AND SEE IF YOU DON'T FEEL JUST A BIT BETTER.

JUNE 13

Doing the right thing is its own reward.

Living the Promises

JUNE 14

Don't relax your standards, be relaxed as you uphold them.

There is nothing that makes people doubt our convictions more than our insistence that people see, hear, appreciate, and agree with them.

LET YOUR JOY IN HAVING THEM SPEAK FOR ITSELF.

JUNE 15

Me: "I get to believe in whatever?"

Sponsor: "Yes."

Me: "Really?"

Sponsor: "Yes."

Me: "But I don't know what to believe in."

Sponsor: "Start by believing that I believe—in you and your ability to do this sobriety thing."

AND IN THE BEGINNING, THAT WAS ALL I HAD AND ALL I NEEDED TO PUT ONE FOOT IN FRONT OF THE OTHER, ONE DAY AT A TIME.

JUNE 16

> We have been given an energy and enthusiasm borne of our Higher Power, with which to greet each day.

When we first tap into that energy, and the enthusiasm that comes with it (you know, when we just can't stop talking about how amazing this program and its blessings are), they call it being on our "pink cloud."

And while not all days are as rosy as others, if I fall off my cloud that doesn't mean I can't climb right back on it if I choose.

I KIND OF LIKE THE VIEW FROM UP THERE.

JUNE 17

What is the "big fiction" that prevents you from reaching your fullest potential, for your own sake as well as those you might impact?

Typically, it's the story you've made up in your mind that says you're "not enough."

But not enough of what? To achieve what goal?

Rewrite your "story" by identifying the gap between where you are and where you want to be, and then go to work on what is needed to close that gap.

IF YOU WANT SOMETHING BADLY ENOUGH, YOU WILL FIND MORE THAN ENOUGH IN YOU AND AROUND YOU TO MAKE IT HAPPEN.

Living the Promises

JUNE 18

Suffering doesn't necessarily come from circumstances themselves; it comes mostly from how we react to them.

We don't have to pretend things don't hurt.

We also don't have to hang on to hurt to prove that we care.

We can look at whether or not the emotion we inject into the situation actually serves us and choose a better one if it doesn't.

THAT'S THE BEAUTY OF A CLEAN, CLEAR, AND SOBER MIND.

JUNE 19

It's not up to me to decide what a win looks like for you in sobriety.

It's up to you to find your sober victories.

IT'S UP TO ME TO HELP YOU CELEBRATE THEM.

JUNE 20

If my level of intensity is always a "10," if I'm always on high alert, I will never develop the wisdom to know the difference between what I can change and what I can't.

Life doesn't have to frantically happen a certain way (my way), in a certain time frame (all at once, preferably yesterday).

Not everything is urgent.

Knowing that, I will take my time, think things through, and more carefully consider my options.

I'M MORE RELAXED JUST THINKING ABOUT IT.

JUNE 21

Making sound choices, doing the right thing, isn't just about us in that time and circumstance; sharing the results also confirms to others the overall soundness of our path.

New people need to hear and **see** the specifics of how well this program works if we work it.

SHOW UP AND SHARE YOUR SOLUTIONS TODAY.

Living the Promises

JUNE 22

Be gracious and kind, without condition, remembering the difference it makes when you receive the same.

We remember the nervous relief and gratitude we felt from being welcomed unconditionally when we arrived.

WE COMMIT TO GIVING OTHERS THAT SAME GIFT, IN AND OUT OF THE ROOMS.

JENIFER M

JUNE 23

If I insist on being the center of attention, I pray that it's for the right reason.

Which is to benefit others.

PERIOD.

JUNE 24

Just because some can't see the dreadful wrecks we were in the wonderful people we've become doesn't mean an extraordinary transformation hasn't occurred.

WE REALLY DON'T HAVE TO DRAG PIECES OF OUR OLD LIFE AROUND TO PROVE HOW FAR WE'VE COME.

JUNE 25

My ego doesn't prop me up, it just holds me up.

When we are in full-on ego mode, we tend to exaggerate, complicate, and aggravate everyone and everything.

It totally gets in the way of being up to bigger and better things.

TODAY IS A GOOD DAY TO GIVE MY EGO A BREAK.

JUNE 26

Everyone has their moments of doubt and pain, but chasing negative thoughts, indulging them, only leads to inevitably darker conclusions.

I used to play the "what if" game to exhaustion.

And since I completely doubted my abilities, the conclusion was never a happy one.

But time and work in the program proves that we have way more resources than we ever imagined, so today, if I'm going to chase a "what if" scenario, it will be for the sake of learning to create solid contingency plans.

THEN I CAN TURN THE PLAN AND THE RESULTS OVER TO MY HIGHER POWER, KNOWING THAT THE ANSWERS WILL REVEAL THEMSELVES.

JENIFER M

JUNE 27

Find your faith, and when you do, put it to good use.

JUNE 28

I graciously accept what is mine to receive, and happily let go of what will be of better service elsewhere.

TO ME, THAT'S WHAT IT MEANS TO GO WITH THE FLOW.

JUNE 29

Idealism kept me focused on a better future long enough for the talk to become the walk.

I was too cynical in the beginning to believe much about the promise of the program, but I sure believed that you believed it.

Still, I thought you were all talk.

But I believed just enough in the basic ideal of peace and serenity and promise, to keep coming back as suggested, and to listen to the difference it was making in your life to be so proactive.

Your excitement about your progress lit a spark for me; I had to take action too.

And as I took more and more action, I became on fire for the real changes I experienced in my mind, body, and soul—changes I was no longer just reading about or watching in others.

THANKS FOR SETTING ME ABLAZE.

Living the Promises

JUNE 30

Center.

208 — JENIFER M

july

"Self-seeking will slip away."

JULY 1

Ever the curious one, the first time I worked on this concept with my sponsor I was loaded with questions: "What does self-seeking really mean? How does it slip away? Does it come back? Do we never, ever worry about ourselves again? How is that possible?"

Ever the patient woman, she said:

"It means choosing only for you, at all costs.

"It slips away as you clear the wreckage of your past and become willing to make your life about something bigger than you.

"It only returns when you relax your standard of bettering yourself for the sake of who you might benefit."

SHE WAS A WISE WOMAN, THAT ONE.

JULY 2

Be mindful of becoming too cynical in response to life's challenges; it clouds your vision and darkens your spirit.

We also don't have to go to the other extreme of blue-sky optimism and deny our difficulties.

BEING MOSTLY SUNNY IS PROBABLY OUR BEST BET FOR WEATHERING LIFE'S UPS AND DOWNS.

JULY 3

People typically do the best they can with what they've got, on any given day. Cutting them a little slack—letting them be fellow, fallible humans—may be the order of the day.

When someone is being especially difficult, their fussiness may purely be a byproduct of feeling overwhelmed and out of resources.

Rather than faulting them for being that way, ask how you can support them.

CHANCES ARE, NO ONE HAS REACHED OUT TO THEM LIKE THAT LATELY.

JULY 4

Judge your worth by the right measure...

...BY HOW MUCH YOU GIVE RATHER THAN GAIN, BY HOW MUCH YOU CAN SERVE RATHER THAN DEMAND.

JULY 5

One of the most beautiful gifts of my sobriety is the ability to feel genuine, heartfelt enthusiasm for another's success, to no longer be in the grip of envy.

We can feel it when envy takes hold: we feel small, inadequate, possessive, and scarce.

But if we examine those feelings closely, most of them don't match the reality of the infinite blessings in our lives.

Nothing else has hold of us at that time but a part of our mind that says the world and its opportunities are limited.

OPEN YOUR HEART AND YOUR MIND TO THE INFINITE GRACE OF YOUR HIGHER POWER, AND YOU WILL ONCE AGAIN KNOW ABUNDANCE.

Living the Promises

JULY

6

To live your best life, find delight in who you are, apart from what you have or do.

As an exercise in confidently stating your best qualities, find at least ten ways to finish this statement with words that positively describe your emotional, intellectual, and spiritual being:

"I am...."

(PS, A THESAURUS MAY COME IN HANDY.)

(PPS, FEEDBACK FROM A FEW TRUSTED FRIENDS MIGHT HELP AS WELL.)

JULY 7

Rising above small thought and petty actions doesn't make us better than everyone else, it just makes us better.

And it makes others better, on some level, by the example it sets.

WHETHER WE KNOW IT OR NOT.

JULY 8

Everything worthwhile in my life has been accomplished the same way sobriety has: with faith, determined effort, and a ton of support, one day at a time.

I tried using faint hope, but without deep faith and resolve to fuel my actions, my goals were just pipe dreams.

I made halfhearted efforts filled with doubt, and got disappointing results.

I tried to do it alone, and ended up in bad company.

I tried to avoid the hard parts, and only do what I wanted instead of what was needed, and totally missed the mark.

I projected the worst, instead of visualizing the best.

REVERSE ALL THAT, AND YOU'VE GOT A PRETTY GOOD FORMULA FOR SUCCESS.

JENIFER M

JULY 9

> I have never regretted doing the right thing. I whined about it maybe, selfishly wished I didn't have to go through the pain of it, but never regretted it.

I've regretted a whole lot of things I've said and done in my life, especially in my addiction.

ACTING WITH INTEGRITY WAS NEVER ONE OF THEM.

JULY 10

> My sobriety took great leaps forward when I started relating to our common human conditions instead of trying to find myself in everyone's stories.

We don't walk in to this program geared to look for the similarities over the differences.

We are typically looking for reasons we might not actually be alcoholics or addicts, any sign that we're not one of "those people."

But if we stick around, we find it is more important to relate to the cause of our misery than the effect it had.

Then we discover that being "one of them" and sharing in their solution can forever release us from our misery.

IT'S NOT SUCH A BAD TRADE-OFF.

JULY 11

> Best advice my mother gave me (although neither of us knew it at the time): "Jenifer, pay attention. Open your eyes, and watch where you're going."

I thought moving blindly through life was part of being creative, spontaneous, and carefree.

TURNS OUT IT WAS MORE CARELESS THAN ANYTHING.

JULY 12

Imagine the impact of showing up for life as though everything was already exactly as you'd like it to be.

Being content with your life doesn't necessarily mean you're being complacent or that you see no room for improvement.

Being content is appreciating your life in the moment while still taking an active role in its progress.

Being content is not about being lazy; it's about being relaxed and grateful while you push on.

NO MATTER WHAT.

JULY 13

My ego kept me in the rooms until my Higher Power could get me sober.

Having been a professional entertainer during my active addiction, once I got clean and sober enough to get my energy back, I "performed" in meetings. I was quite impressed with how quickly I memorized the literature, and could recite "how it works" and give program advice, and by how excited people seemed to be to see me.

I'm sure it was only mildly amusing for people to watch, especially the old-timers.

Thankfully, I stuck around long enough that my Higher Power could break through and break down all that ego.

IT TOOK MORE THAN A FEW LESSONS IN HUMILITY TO STOP SHOWING OFF AND JUST START SHOWING UP.

JULY 14

Share your gratitude and happiness in a way that inspires others to find their own.

Don't be afraid to share the victories of your recovery: **NOT TO BRAG, BUT TO HELP.**

JULY 15

Sponsor: "If you want to stop saying you're sorry, then stop doing things to be sorry for."

That advice was a little too simplistic for me when I first got it.

See, I had good reasons for everything I did, and I believed that if "you people" would work a little harder to understand and appreciate my choices, I wouldn't have to apologize so much.

SORRY ABOUT THAT.

Living the Promises

JULY 16

Today is a good day to stop being righteously indignant about the problems of the world and to focus more intently on doing my part to solve them.

It may seem like there is no end to the evils of the world.

And maybe it will take untold lifetimes for good to finally win out.

But in the meantime, we're here, in this space and time, and we can make a real difference, one thought at a time, one choice at a time, one day at a time.

IT'S A GOOD FIGHT TO FIGHT.

JULY 17

We are each "enough": we don't need to make up stories about ourselves to be worthy of love, grace, and recovery.

JULY 18

> By thoroughly working these steps, we not only get to pinpoint the exact nature of our wrongs, we also get to reveal our vast and beautiful spirit.

Taking inventory, especially the first time, doesn't exactly feel like a "get to," more like a "have to."

Which tends to elicit pleadings like, "Ugh, do I have to?"

Inventory doesn't really become a "get to" until we get through it once or twice and discover that no one will run screaming from the room upon hearing it, that each time we face our past, it loses a little more power over us, and that an extraordinary new version of us takes its place.

TO "PINPOINT" OUR DEFECTS MEANS WE GET TO LOOK DIRECTLY AT THEM; WE NO LONGER HAVE TO—OR WANT TO—TURN AWAY.

JENIFER M

JULY 19

Being "happy, joyous, and free" in your sobriety depends on bringing as much life and energy to your program as you envision it bringing to you.

Staying clean and sober is work: hard work, joyous work, exhausting, uplifting, life-altering work.

And doing the work doesn't just change us for the better physically and mentally; it forever improves our heart and our spirit.

YOU ARE WORTH WORKING FOR, BODY, MIND, AND SOUL.

JULY 20

They got it wrong when they said it's better to ask for forgiveness than for permission.

I used to just come to, and make snap decisions about what I selfishly needed and wanted.

I was rarely concerned with asking for permission or forgiveness.

I am grateful to now be awake to the potential consequences of my actions, and therefore more thoughtful in my conduct.

POLITE, RESPECTFUL, AND UNASSUMING GOES A LONG WAY IN THIS LIFE.

JULY 21

Everything we need to stay clean and sober is just a request, a meeting, a prayer away.

JULY 22

Acting in opposition to our core values pits us against our better nature and puts us in danger of compromising very important parts of our life, including what keeps us sober.

Here's the thing about this program: searching, fearless, thorough examinations of our motives, defects, and secrets gets us really honest.

So honest that it becomes painfully obvious when we consciously choose to be out of integrity with our new standards for living.

The good news is, these steps teach us to think things through before we speak and act, and to do so on more than just our own behalf.

And that is the discipline by which we can cease fighting ourselves, or anyone, any more.

JUST LET YOUR CONSCIENCE BE YOUR GUIDE.

JENIFER M

JULY 23

Taking the cotton out of my ears and sticking it in my mouth, learning to just listen in meetings, was one of my first lessons in how to be a patient observer and enjoy some of the nuances of life for what felt like the very first time.

If we're constantly zipping around, literally or figuratively, we will be too busy to experience the beautiful subtleties of language, movement, and intent that surround us.

IT WOULD BE A SHAME TO MISS THOSE.

JULY 24

These steps taught me how to match a clear mind with proper, helpful conduct, which was my first act of service.

IT HAS BECOME MY BEST ACT OF SERVICE.

—JENIFER M

Create space in your mind for greater possibilities by being wildly curious.

Challenge your thoughts first.

MAKE YOUR MIND UP ABOUT THEM LATER.

JULY
25

JULY 26

Be careful that you don't claim certain behaviors—such as anger, resentment, or arrogance—as your "badge of honor."

If they don't serve the greater good, they are not worth hanging on to.

NONE OF THOSE BEHAVIORS EQUALS REAL POWER ANYWAY.

JULY 27

To know that your enemy has suffered may bring some sense of temporary relief, but only compassion will bring you peace.

JULY 28

It's ok to take some personal pleasure in your accomplishments, as long as your ultimate happiness isn't dependent on them.

Appreciate them.

Be grateful for them.

TRY NOT TO GET TOO ATTACHED TO OR DEFINED BY THEM.

JULY 29

It is a fine day when we realize that our deeds are more useful than our opinions.

I don't need to talk about what I've done to make a difference or need you to throw me a parade for having done so; I just need to do it.

LET THE RESULTS DO THE TALKING.

JULY 30

This program snatches us from the brink of permanent insanity or death and brings us to the verge of a beautiful life by giving us the tools to choose wisely and patiently.

THE REST IS UP TO US,
ONE DAY AT A TIME.

JENIFER M

Breathe.

JULY
31

Living the Promises

august

"Our whole attitude and outlook upon life will change."

AUGUST 1

It has been more than 25 years since I was the lying, thieving, cheat that I had become before I hit bottom in my addiction and started in recovery. Or at least 20 years since I was that gal.

It's definitely been more than 25 years since I was the **DRINKING**, lying, thieving, cheat that I was.

There is a big distinction here, which is that sober doesn't necessarily mean sane, and not drinking doesn't always mean not manipulating.

It took hours and hours upon days and days and months and years of conditioning myself to new standards and values before I could claim a new outlook and attitude on life—one that now moves mostly from a place of love and service.

WHICH FOR THIS ADDICT AND ALCOHOLIC IS ONLY POSSIBLE BY THE GRACE OF WHATEVER GOD IS.

Living the Promises

AUGUST 2

Happiness, peace, and serenity is an inside-out job.

Each of these is a choice and, to be sustainable, must originate from deep within.

And discovery and cultivation of them isn't the only goal.

YOU'VE GOT TO SHARE THEM WITH OTHERS TO HONOR THEM COMPLETELY.

AUGUST 3

Diligence is a small price to pay for the freedom sobriety affords me.

Where else in our lives is so much given in exchange for so little?

THINK ABOUT IT.

AUGUST 4

When I make my decisions from the right place to start with—from service, not self, from faith and not fear...

...THEN THE REST OF THE DETAILS SEEM TO MAGICALLY SORT THEMSELVES OUT.

— JENIFER M

"Be careful what you pray for, you just might get it."

Unless I'm praying for the strength to contribute to the happiness of others, in which case I don't have to be careful in asking.

I ONLY HAVE TO BE CAREFUL NOT TO GET TOO ATTACHED TO A CERTAIN VERSION OF THE OUTCOME.

AUGUST 5

AUGUST 6

Let your decisions inform you before, during, and after the fact.

A lot of things worked out in my life
in spite of me and my addiction.

I was lucky that way.

But eventually my luck ran out, and then it
was time to take an active role in my success.

I did that by learning how to learn;
silly as it seems, being strategic wasn't
something I knew how to do.

I started by asking some very
basic questions throughout the
process of making big decisions.

Before: What goal am I after?
How will I get there?

During: How is it going?
What will I change?

After: How did it go?
Would I go there again and why or why not?

**IT'S A METHOD THAT HAS
PREVENTED A WHOLE LOT OF
UNNECESSARY INSANITY.**

AUGUST 7

Open up and it adds up.

I can sit in meetings and hope to hear my solutions, or I can tell on myself and really get some feedback.

ONCE I OPEN UP, I'M GUARANTEED TO HAVE A WHOLE BUNCH OF PERSPECTIVES TO CHOOSE FROM.

AUGUST 8

Get out of self and give what you can—it all matters.

There's no such thing as a small act of self.

Every time we make the effort to get out of our own way and give to another, we have set things in motion that can result in something bigger and more beautiful than we can imagine.

THINK OF IT LIKE THE BEAT OF THE BUTTERFLY WING ON ONE SIDE OF THE WORLD THAT CAN CREATE A TSUNAMI ON THE OTHER.

AUGUST 9

> We create this connection out of a deep relation to not only our pain, but also to our amazement for our transformation—we know each other on a level few others can.

I never cease to be amazed at our willingness to reach out to complete strangers who share our affliction and offer our love, support, and kindness, as true friends, as though it's always been so.

NOW THAT'S A MIRACLE.

AUGUST 10

I asked God to remove the obsession and compulsion, and I promised to do the rest of the footwork.

SO FAR, WE'VE EACH HELD UP OUR ENDS OF THE BARGAIN.

JENIFER M

AUGUST 11

"Smooth sailing" takes strong intention and a calm mind.

It is not only through our struggles that we grow.

It takes as much—if not more—discipline and practice to be steady and even-keeled.

IT TAKES A LITTLE BIT OF WORK SOMETIMES TO RELAX AND ENJOY THE RIDE.

AUGUST 12

I came, I came to, I came to believe...

I CAME TO LIFE.

— JENIFER M

AUGUST 13

It's ok to be reasonable, practical, and sane.

It doesn't necessarily make us less interesting.

IT MIGHT EVEN MAKE US HAPPIER AND MORE HELPFUL.

AUGUST 14

Don't give people permission to rock your boat.

YOU HAVE THAT CHOICE TODAY.

AUGUST 15

Sponsor: "Never take advice from someone who is doing worse than you are. Learn from them, but don't take their counsel except as a cautionary tale."

I had to learn how to tell who those people were, the ones who had all the answers but didn't really know the questions.

I wasn't looking for people to be perfect, but I was hopeful that they were at least walking their talk.

I kept studying them and found out that some were, some weren't.

IT TAKES SOME TIME, AND SOME CAREFUL OBSERVATION, AND YOU WILL LEARN TO DISCERN THE DIFFERENCE.

AUGUST 16

What does it mean to deepen?

To deepen our understanding of something means opening ourselves up to a full experience of it.

By doing so, we allow the thoughts in our head and the feelings in our gut to meet up with the intuition of our heart.

THIS IS HOW WE CREATE AN UNDERSTANDING ON A CELLULAR LEVEL, ONE SO INGRAINED AS TO FOREVER BE A PART OF US.

AUGUST 17

Never forget what got you here.

If we are doing the work, we no longer have to fear or regret our past.

WE DO HAVE TO REMEMBER AND RESPECT IT.

AUGUST 18

Gratitude (My 2nd Top 10 List):

To laugh.
To create.
To care.
To learn.
To lead.
To imagine.
To dream.
To pray.
To play.
TO LOVE.

AUGUST 19

Leadership is the ability to inspire others to greatness while making room for their failings.

No one got to their goals without a few missteps along the way.

Nor did they get there without people who not only made room for their mistakes, but also helped them see and celebrate what an important part they play in the process.

IT'S NOT AN EXCUSE TO BE LAZY THOUGH.

AUGUST 20

To love is to make oneself completely available to the full expression of another's spirit.

Working the 12 Steps teaches us to be equally present to people's joys and their sorrows.

It teaches us to go beyond the idea or fantasy of love to actually being loving.

I LOVE THAT.

AUGUST 21

We can look to the present to predict our future: our choices today will all manifest some day, in ways big and small, for better or for worse.

What we can't know is when, where, or how they will manifest.

But knowing that someday they will, we can at least be more mindful of our choices in the present.

IT'S THE GENERAL CONCEPT OF KARMA.

AUGUST 22

Don't let fear of relapse prevent you from living life.

There's healthy fear, and not-so-healthy fear.

Healthy fear keeps us from putting ourselves with people, places, and things that endanger our sobriety. It reminds us to look both ways before we cross the street, if you will.

Unhealthy fear keeps us paralyzed and isolated, which prevents us from developing the skills to be a contributing member of society.

If we honor and uphold what keeps us clean and sober, then we won't have to retreat from the world.

THAT'S WHAT IT MEANS TO BE FREE.

JENIFER M

AUGUST 23

In our mad rush to make sense of difficult circumstances, we often assign meaning to them that is neither accurate nor useful. Better to settle down and sort through the details with an open, curious, and patient mind.

We are so bound and determined to identify and explain things that we often miss the chance to see them for what they really are.

So instead of automatically deciding what "it" is, ask yourself (and make time to contemplate the answers to), "What could 'it' be?"

THE MERE ACT OF SLOWING DOWN ENOUGH TO CONSIDER THE ALTERNATIVES IS USUALLY ENOUGH TO GET THE PERSPECTIVE YOU NEED TO ACT FROM A POSITION OF STRENGTH.

AUGUST 24

We don't need to get too attached to external validation—our goodness is proven by its own expression.

AUGUST 25

Don't react to someone else's negativity as though it's your first—or last—encounter with it.

Or as though you've never experienced or expressed your own negativity.

See it for whatever it is, as best as you can, and work with a desire to improve or learn from it.

THEN YOU CAN MOVE ON FROM IT.

AUGUST 26

When it comes to working my recovery program, as my dad would say, "I laugh and joke, but I don't play!"

I have had great fun in my sobriety.

I have also been through some really hard times, most of my own making.

Bankruptcy, foreclosure, lost a business, lost some friends.

Lost my father to cancer.

Through it all, I remembered to do the simple things that would keep my sobriety intact.

Meetings, sponsorship, inventory, amends, and a whole lot of prayer.

Sobriety had to be first, always, no matter how bad I felt.

Because life happens and I need to do my part to stay steady through it all.

YOU GAVE ME THOSE TOOLS; I JUST HAD TO KEEP THEM CLOSE.

JENIFER M

AUGUST 27

There is a powerful difference between what we take in and what we take on: one informs us, the other defines us.

When I treated others as though what they had to say was gospel, I took on more of their opinions, moods, and directives than was necessary.

If you were in a bad mood, it had to have been because of something I said or did.

If you expressed an opinion forcefully enough, I couldn't help but be swayed a little.

If you told me what to do with any amount of certainty, I probably did it.

You didn't ask me to take all that on; I did it without realizing I was doing it; I did it because I didn't trust my own opinion and intuition.

Today, through a lot of trial and error, I have enough experience to know what works for me and what doesn't. I can let you be who and how you want to be without making it all about me.

SO HAPPY TO FINALLY HAVE A MIND OF MY OWN. I'LL BET YOU ARE TOO.

AUGUST 28

Leave room for redemption—yours and others'.

We shouldn't judge people based on a single snapshot of their life any more than we would want them to do that to us.

Everyone has as much potential for positive change as the next person.

BESIDES, WHO AM I TO JUDGE WHETHER SOMEONE ELSE IS WORTHY OF GOD'S GRACE?

JENIFER M

AUGUST 29

Commune with us.

The meeting before the meeting, the meeting after the meeting, and the picnics, parties, and holiday gatherings with others in recovery all provide a wonderful opportunity to learn to socialize.

These are the occasions where you can study how people interact with others, look for qualities and skill sets you want to emulate, and learn to build great rapport with others.

It's where I learned how to not just amuse or entertain people, but to really connect with them.

IT IS WHERE I LEARNED TO LET PEOPLE IN.

Living the Promises

AUGUST 30

There's what's in our steps and traditions, and then there is all the other stuff we added to that.

When in doubt about how to proceed, pick up our program book and **FOLLOW THE BLACK PRINT ON THE WHITE PAGE**.

Pray.

AUGUST
31

Living the Promises

september

"Fear of people and of economic insecurity will leave us."

SEPTEMBER 1

> Of course I was afraid of you—when I got sober I didn't trust myself and my own motives, so I sure didn't trust you or yours. But the more trustworthy I became, and the purer my motives got, the less I feared others.

And at the end of the day, what's to fear in someone else anyway?

Underneath the trappings of money, property, or prestige is just another person trying to get along in the world, trying to find love, security, and peace, just like me.

As for money, you never said I wouldn't experience economic insecurity; you promised I wouldn't fear it. And sure enough, because of the practical steps you gave me for staying on top of things financially, I have had fewer surprises in that area.

Circumstances maybe, challenges certainly, but very little that I can't see coming.

WHICH GOES FOR PEOPLE AND MONEY, COME TO THINK OF IT.

Living the Promises

SEPTEMBER 2

Stop saying "I'm trying," and start saying "I'm doing."

We have more than enough tools to keep us sober and serene each day.

Sometimes it feels like too many choices; when we're feeling lost or really off the beam, sometimes we get stuck trying to pick the "right" one or the "best" one.

Our best bet in those moments is to decide that each tool is as good as the other.

Oh, and to pick one up and use it.

And if that tool doesn't do the trick, to use another.

And another.

And another.

UNTIL WE FIND WHAT WORKS.

JENIFER M

SEPTEMBER 3

Detaching—with love—from certain people, places, and things doesn't mean I no longer care; it just means I'm no longer at their mercy.

When others are careening around in their drama and anguish, I don't have to go along for the ride just to prove my concern.

AS A MATTER OF FACT, I AM PROBABLY A WHOLE LOT MORE USEFUL AS THE DESIGNATED DRIVER OF CALM, AS IT WERE.

SEPTEMBER 4

Unconditional love is not without its boundaries.

No matter how crazy I was in my addiction, my family kept loving me.

WHAT SAVED MY LIFE IS WHEN THEY STOPPED PUTTING UP WITH ME.

JENIFER M

SEPTEMBER

Pride is a curious thing.

At its best, pride is the happy confidence we express once we have reclaimed our dignity.

At its worst, it is the arrogance and vanity that is at the root of "self-will run riot."

Two sides, same coin.

IT'S NOT HARD TO SEE WHICH SIDE IT'S BETTER TO BE ON.

SEPTEMBER 6

To the God of my understanding: thank you for revealing yourself and for lighting the way to a clean, clear, sober, and joyous life.

SEPTEMBER 7

> Our literature was divinely inspired; we owe it to ourselves and our sobriety to go beneath the surface of the words to find the depth of life-saving instruction within them.

Study the material; don't just skim it.

Internalize the lesson; don't just intellectualize it.

Experience the blessing; don't just expound on it.

AND THEN CARRY THE MESSAGE TO EVERYONE YOU CAN.

Living the Promises

SEPTEMBER 8

There, but for the grace of God, go I...

and here, by the grace of God, am I.

GRACE WHICH, BY THE WAY, IS THERE FOR THE ASKING FOR ANYONE AND EVERYONE WHO HAS A SINCERE DESIRE FOR IT.

SEPTEMBER 9

> We don't have to know how many minutes, hours, or days it will take for things to improve; we simply have to have faith that they will.

Which doesn't mean we sit idly in a corner somewhere waiting for change to arrive; we go after it.

And there are times that we will stop dead in our tracks because we won't want to go another step without a guarantee of where it will take us.

But there are no guarantees in life, only possibilities and probabilities.

TAKE ADVANTAGE OF THE POSSIBILITIES BY THOROUGHLY FOLLOWING THE PATH, AND YOU ARE VERY, VERY LIKELY TO MEET WITH SUCCESS ALONG THE WAY.

SEPTEMBER 10

> Thank God—whatever God is—that there is room in this program for a God of my understanding.

In the beginning, I resisted the notion of God and only chose a version that was just enough to keep me sober that day.

I wasn't particularly interested in a lifelong commitment.

Seeing God as Good Orderly Direction worked just fine, for a while, but it was still only a halfhearted concession.

But on my darkest day in sobriety, the only thing that ultimately stood between me and a drink was a power greater than what I could name.

The feeling of God working in my life in that moment got so personal and so big that I couldn't explain it; I only had time to embrace it.

I've never been worried about what to call it since.

THANKS FOR GIVING ME PLENTY OF ROOM TO WORK THAT OUT.

JENIFER M

SEPTEMBER 11

We get no clarity until we get calm.

THE HEAT OF THE MOMENT IS NO TIME TO MAKE UP MY MIND.

SEPTEMBER 12

Today we can face our fear, doubt, pain, or anger—we don't have to indulge or relive it.

Indulging it or reliving it is a choice, not a given.

Facing it means examining it for what I can learn from it, and then letting it go.

I know, easier said than done.

UNLESS YOU PRACTICE IT, AND THEN IT BECOMES MORE EASILY SAID AND DONE.

SEPTEMBER 13

Enjoy the victories in recovery, linger with them a while, but don't languish.

We can't afford to rest on our laurels because our disease is constantly on the move, ready to take our lives back over the moment we let up on maintaining a "fit spiritual condition."

WE DON'T NEED TO BE PARANOID ABOUT IT, JUST VIGILANT.

SEPTEMBER 14

Prayer is...

a conversation;

a request;

a review;

an acknowledgment;

a connection.

IT'S NOT MEANT TO BE A NEGOTIATION.

SEPTEMBER 15

Sponsor: "Just because sobriety doesn't always feel good, doesn't mean it isn't working. You've got growing pains, and if you work this program, you will finally grow up.

"Keep working it and your times of joy will outweigh your times of pain and uncertainty."

IT FEELS GOOD TO FINALLY BE A GROWN-UP.

SEPTEMBER 16

Pay attention to the still, small voice inside that will lead you away from the mistakes of the past and toward a brighter future.

SEPTEMBER 17

Staying clean and sober isn't rocket science.

It just feels that way sometimes.

We often feel compelled to complicate the heck out of it, but no one said that was necessary.

AS A MATTER OF FACT, I THINK THEY SAY "KEEP IT SIMPLE" BECAUSE IT REALLY, TRULY, ALREADY IS.

SEPTEMBER 18

Imagine where we would be today without the family, friends, sponsors, fellow travelers, coaches, teachers, and strangers who have been brave enough to call us on our "stuff."

Or if we hadn't finally been brave enough to accept the help.

BOY, HAVE I GOT SOME THANK-YOU NOTES TO WRITE.

SEPTEMBER 19

As powerful as the steps, meetings, and traditions is the love and support of openhearted, closed-mouthed friends.

I have found nothing more therapeutic than laying out my defects and challenges in a room full of people who "get" me, knowing that they will work to help me find a solution.

They may not always get it right, but they are always right there when I need them.

WHAT A BLESSING.

SEPTEMBER 20

Whether we are stepping back from a ledge of fear or climbing out of a well of self-pity, a true desire for peace and serenity will lead us back to that central place in our hearts where God lives.

JENIFER M

SEPTEMBER 21

The day begins, like any other day, and by virtue of being clean, sober, and clear, you get to have a bigger and better hand than ever in how it turns out.

You can pick your attitude.

You can pick your battles.

You can pick your friends.

You can pick your sponsor.

You can pick a meeting.

You can pick the God of your understanding.

HOW COOL IS THAT?

Living the Promises

SEPTEMBER 22

"We admitted that we were powerless…"

"Admitting" got me through the doors—acceptance kept me in the rooms.

But even though I could admit I drank too much, I couldn't quite admit that I was powerless over it.

That is, until things got bad enough that I could come to no other conclusion.

Being able to admit it still didn't equal automatic acceptance of the idea.

Acceptance took time; a lot of time.

Fortunately, as long as I could admit my powerlessness, I stood a chance of finding acceptance and then solutions.

SURPRISINGLY, VERY LITTLE OF THIS TRANSFORMATION WAS AN INTELLECTUAL PROCESS; IT WAS MORE LIKE A GRADUAL CHANGE OF HEART.

JENIFER M

SEPTEMBER 23

> Once I admitted—and accepted—my powerlessness over alcohol and drugs, I had to eventually admit and accept that same powerlessness over people, places, and things.

Believe it or not, the second part was harder than the first because I had lived for so long with the delusion that being able to negatively influence and manipulate people equaled control over them.

It didn't. It only meant I had a finely tuned radar for finding people who would allow themselves to be pushed around.

The healthy ones, the ones who weren't so willing to be manipulated, were the ones who helped shatter my illusion by refusing to bend to my will.

THANK GOODNESS THEY STOOD SO STRONG, OR I MIGHT NEVER HAVE KNOWN THE DIFFERENCE.

Living the Promises

SEPTEMBER 24

"...that our lives had become unmanageable."

Now there's an understatement.

No problems admitting to that one.

Taking responsibility for it, now that's a different story.

WHEN WE CAN DO THAT, WE ARE FREE TO FIND MANAGEABILITY.

JENIFER M

(At my first anniversary)

Me: "This thing really works!"

Sponsor: "I told you so."

BEST "I TOLD YOU SO" EVER.

SEPTEMBER 25

SEPTEMBER 26

"Came to believe…"

Which took a crazy combination of

pushing and pulling,

prodding and inviting,

resistance and surrender,

skepticism and faith.

NOBODY MADE ME, BUT THANK GOODNESS THEY ENCOURAGED ME.

SEPTEMBER 27

"...restore us to sanity."

As crazy as our lives are by the time we get clean and sober, you'd think we would jump all over the idea of regaining some sanity.

Unfortunately, that's not always the case.

Especially if we think that to be sane means to live a boring, mundane, and uninspiring life.

For me, nothing could have been further from the truth. I'm not sure if I was restored to sanity so much as introduced to it, but either way, the sanity that came into my life by working the 12 Steps created a stable ground from which I could grow beyond my wildest dreams.

SANITY THEN CAME TO MEAN EXERCISING COMMON SENSE WHILE KEEPING A WICKED SENSE OF HUMOR AND LIVING LIFE TO THE FULLEST.

Living the Promises

SEPTEMBER 28

"Made a searching and fearless moral inventory…"

It's important not to rush this step, especially the first time through.

The instructions are simple enough; the guides are right there in the step itself.

It's the searching, fearless, and moral part that's not so easy.

But get it out of your head, and on paper, and you will begin to see the truth of where you've been, the impact it had on others, your part in it, and how best to improve.

THAT IS, IF YOU USE YOUR INVENTORY AS AN OPPORTUNITY TO GAIN WISDOM, RATHER THAN JUST SOMETHING TO WHIP YOURSELF WITH.

SEPTEMBER 29

"Admitted to God, to ourselves, and to another human being the exact nature of our wrongs."

It is unmistakably freeing to unburden ourselves, out loud, in front of God and a closed-mouth friend, for the sake of growth and continued sobriety.

IT REALLY, REALLY IS.

SEPTEMBER 30

Lighten up.

october

> "We will intuitively know how to handle situations which used to baffle us."

OCTOBER 1

At some point in my recovery it dawned on me, in the most beautiful, revelatory way, that I could finally trust my intuition.

In my addiction, what little insight I had was buried under the obsession and compulsion for how to meet the day's cravings.

Upon getting clean and sober, I not only worked the steps to clear the wreckage of my past, but also of my mind. I learned to be calm, to trust the God of my understanding, to pray, and to meditate, and as a result, I was able to experience a level of awareness I had never known.

Over time, my intuition has grown stronger and stronger, and I have developed a keener sense than ever of where and how I can best serve others.

This commitment to service, particularly on behalf of other alcoholics and addicts, wasn't what I set out to do in recovery; by doing the work, it slowly but surely became what my heart is set on.

AND WITH SERVICE AS MY FIRST FOCUS, THERE IS PRACTICALLY NOTHING LEFT TO BE BAFFLED ABOUT.

Living the Promises

OCTOBER 2

> If I do the work, my character defects will transform from being driving forces that I can't control, to petty annoyances for which I have a clear solution.

It's hard to let go of our character defects: they provide a shelter of sorts, a hiding place, a little box in which to wrap the questionable behavior that we can't explain or don't want to claim.

And the hard truth is, we are never fully rid of our defects.

But with a little luck, and a lot of work, we can at least learn to recognize them the moment they arise, and then quickly set them aside in favor of our strengths.

WHETHER WE CHOOSE TO DO SO OR NOT IS UP TO US.

JENIFER M

OCTOBER 3

Insanity: thinking I could go through all that inventory work but hang on to my defects and still experience "happy, joyous, and free."

Evidently, being "entirely ready" to have our defects removed takes some of us a little longer than others.

I SAID I WAS SMART WHEN I CAME INTO THE PROGRAM; I DIDN'T SAY I HAD A CLUE.

OCTOBER 4

Lifting my defects up to God—over and over—and taking them back—again and again—was quite the workout.

Even after I got clean and sober, I still caused a lot of damage with my defects; it took quite a while to realize the folly in hanging on to the deadweight that they were.

Eventually, after a ton of unnecessary misery, I tired of that exercise in futility.

I NEVER FELT SO LIGHT AS I DID WHEN I FINALLY LET GO.

OCTOBER 5

Amends, you say? A list of all persons I've harmed?

It is usually quite a list.

But it's not about the number of people who turn up on that list; what matters is the quality of our desire to make things right with them, as best as we can.

And if we miss putting some of these folks on our list the first time through this step, like everything else in this program, we can go back a second time—or a third or a fourth—until we've identified everyone we can who should be on it.

THAT'S ONE OF THE BEAUTIES OF HAVING THIS PROGRAM FOR LIFE.

OCTOBER 6

"Made direct amends…"

Being direct wasn't exactly my forte.

I was a little more used to skirting things.

So my first time through the 9th Step, my sponsor made sure that I actually practiced out loud what a direct amends might sound like before actually making the amends.

Then, with her in my head, and God in my heart, I went forth to make them.

I HAD NO IDEA YOU COULD ROLE-PLAY YOUR WAY TO RELIEF.

JENIFER M

OCTOBER 7

"Continued to take personal inventory…"

My process of inventory today is the same as it was in the very beginning. I start with some very basic reminders:

Q: What is a sign that I need to take inventory?
A: The sun is setting.

Q: What do I inventory?
A: The day and my part in it, good and bad.

Q: Who do I owe an amends?
A: Anyone and everyone I've harmed.

Q: When will I make that amends?
A: As quickly as possible.

THEN I FILL IN THE DETAILS.

OCTOBER 8

"Sought through prayer and meditation to improve..."

The only thing I know for sure is that God's will (whatever God is), is that I better myself for the sake of who I can help.

THE REST IS JUST DETAILS ON WHO, WHAT, WHERE, WHEN, AND HOW.

JENIFER M

OCTOBER 9

"Having had a spiritual awakening..."

By working these steps, we awaken to

freedom,

happiness,

awareness,

service,

serenity,

peace,

helpfulness,

compassion,

intuition,

sincerity,

diligence...

...GOD.

Living the Promises

OCTOBER 10

Be on the lookout for self-obsession: the thoughts, language, and actions that are masquerading as helpful.

You may think you're trying to help someone, but it is important to check in and really be sure if you're doing it for them or for you.

IF YOU'RE NOT SURE, BACK AWAY, AND COME BACK WHEN YOU'VE FOUND THE BEST PERSON FOR THE JOB, WHETHER OR NOT IT'S YOU.

OCTOBER 11

Start the day...

with ease of movement,

an easy mind,

and an easy spirit,

AND SEE IF THE DAY ISN'T JUST A BIT EASIER AS A RESULT.

OCTOBER 12

Start the day over...

if you feel your body,

your mind,

and your spirit

TIGHTENING UP.

OCTOBER 13

End the day...

as you began;

with balance,

perspective,

AND SERENITY.

OCTOBER 14

"Why me?" isn't nearly as important a question as "What now?"

It's not unusual for us to lament the fact that we are addicts and alcoholics.

Or that we've had less-than-ideal childhoods.

Or that our lives today aren't as easy as we'd like them to be.

But all that time with the "why's" of life are only useful if the answers can positively change your future.

IF SO, USE THEM. OTHERWISE, MOVE AWAY FROM "WHY," AND SETTLE IN WITH HOW BEST TO CHANGE FROM HERE.

OCTOBER 15

Sponsor: "If you're willing to fight harder for a wrong decision than for what you know will keep you sober, then you're in trouble."

A SIMPLE, YET PROFOUND GAUGE, NO?

OCTOBER 16

Take your troubles on a little at a time, a day at a time, and look for ways to better yourself through them for the sake of who you can help.

Things will get brighter as you get more determined to push through your challenges.

DON'T LET THE LESSONS IN THEM GO TO WASTE.

OCTOBER 17

A calm mind is the way to greater insight.

The more we settle our thoughts, the more room there is for insight to arise.

And the better our insight, the greater our ability to serve.

And the more we serve, the calmer we feel.

IT'S THE GREAT CIRCLE OF PEACE, WISDOM, AND SERVICE.

OCTOBER 18

Don't join the flock just to have somewhere to be.

One of our most basic human needs is to feel like we belong.

But if we don't examine whether the people, places, and things in our life are a good fit, we risk doing whatever it takes just to fit in.

BE PATIENT, AND YOU WILL FIND YOUR "BIRDS OF A FEATHER."

OCTOBER 19

Get organized.

Open the mail, pay the bills, toss the trash, file the pile, make the bed, straighten the house.

When your surroundings are less cluttered, so is everything else about you.

And the good news is, once you get organized it takes less and less time to stay that way.

WHICH FREES YOU UP FOR ALL THE THINGS YOU WISH YOU COULD DO IF YOU DIDN'T FEEL SO SCATTERED.

Living the Promises

OCTOBER

20

Today I will do more than my "fair share" to see that a newcomer doesn't stay lost in their confusion about how to recover.

There are lots of ways to go beyond sharing to actually reaching out to someone new.

Be a temp sponsor if you can't be a permanent one.

Take the new person to coffee, and share your experience strength and hope one-on-one.

Build extra time in your schedule to hang out after the meeting for a bit and get to know them.

Give them some literature.

Give them your phone number.

Introduce them to someone else at the meeting.

GO THE EXTRA MILE.

JENIFER M

OCTOBER 21

I like my truth today like I used to like my alcohol: straight up and undiluted.

Without the people who have been willing to give me a frank appraisal of my behavior and how it affects others, I probably never would have gotten here.

Much less gotten any better.

But different people receive information different ways: not everyone needs to be beat over the head like I did before they will pay attention to the truth of their addiction and how to recover.

So, if I work to frame the information in a way that can be heard, have the intention to share it with love and to be helpful instead of right, then there is a great chance it will get through, on some level at least.

It's all in the presentation.

THE RESULTS ARE UP TO GOD.

Living the Promises

OCTOBER 22

> There is little room to worry if I'm doing well, if I'm busy wondering how I can do some good.

— JENIFER M

OCTOBER 23

Clear view; clear choice; clear path.

That's the goal, but sometimes all of the above is about as clear as mud.

Now that we're clean and sober, it can be hard to know what we're supposed to do with our lives.

Fortunately, our action plan in sobriety has been laid out very carefully, and has stood the test of time.

We just have to work that plan, one step at a time, one day at a time.

THEN CLARITY, CHOICE, AND PATH IN THE OTHER ASPECTS OF OUR LIFE STAND A BETTER THAN AVERAGE CHANCE OF REVEALING THEMSELVES IN A BETTER THAN AVERAGE WAY.

Living the Promises

OCTOBER 24

Greatness is within us, and always has been, just waiting for us to recognize it.

It is no small feat to do what's necessary to stay clean and sober.

Each day that we accomplish that, we have achieved greatness.

SEE?

OCTOBER 25

"It is what it is."

This phrase is rarely, if ever, used in response to the good times; it is usually reserved to resign ourselves to difficult circumstances.

And we can face the hard reality of those situations now or later, and improve them now or later.

We know that the sooner we face them and decide what to do about them, the sooner we can move onward and upward.

Which leaves us no logical reason to delay.

Except that we're human beings who sometimes prefer denial of the obvious.

So the choice to prolong our misery is just that; our choice.

IT'S THE GOOD NEWS AND THE BETTER NEWS.

Living the Promises

OCTOBER 26

You can't be self-righteous and compassionate at the same time.

And if we insist on such superiority, what we think is compassion can only be pity.

IT IS SO MUCH KINDER, SO MUCH EASIER ON OUR SOUL AND SPIRIT TO RELATE TO OTHERS EMPATHETICALLY.

OCTOBER 27

"Hold your precious little tongue."

One advantage of getting sober in the Deep South was that I had plenty of people that could deliver hard truths in a way that felt like they had just fed me a spoonful of sugar.

One such woman, after tiring of my insistence on talking in every meeting, on every subject (many of which I clearly knew nothing about), decided I needed the above advice.

But she didn't just admonish me; she also suggested that unless I was truly intent on adding to the experience rather than just hearing myself talk, that it could be more helpful to keep my mouth shut.

She was a little scary, in a sweet kind of way.

I guess that's why I paid attention when she told it to me.

EVENTUALLY I EVEN THANKED HER FOR IT.

Living the Promises

OCTOBER 28

"Terminal uniqueness" is an affliction that remains in our system long after the drugs and alcohol have left.

Somehow seeing myself as so special, so remarkable as to be out of reach of anyone's help, only separates me from my solutions.

THERE ARE INFINITELY MORE PRODUCTIVE WAYS TO FEEL.

JENIFER M

OCTOBER 29

"Lost" happens.

We feel lost in sobriety when direction, clarity, and energy have all seemingly failed us.

To regain your energy, reconnect with your motivation for being sober in the first place, and you will invite clarity and direction to return.

And if all else fails, and you just can't find your way alone, **IF YOU HAVE STUCK CLOSE TO THE PEOPLE IN THE PROGRAM, YOU HAVE A BUILT-IN SEARCH PARTY YOU CAN CALL ON FOR HELP.**

OCTOBER 30

Sobriety doesn't give us a pass on pain, but the gift of being present to it.

Remember what it felt like in your addiction to feel insurmountable pain?

To have no answers, only reactions?

To feel victimized by life?

Now remember what it feels like to be out from under that weight, for the fog to have cleared, to have the wherewithal to reach out for help, and to have the vision to see pain for what it is.

To be fully and calmly present to it gives us the strength to move forward from it, and a deeper appreciation for the joys in life.

Because sober or not, pain is a part of life. And we get sober to get our whole lives back, not just the pretty parts.

AND ALL THOSE PARTS ADD UP TO THE STRONG, BEAUTIFUL, SOBER BEINGS THAT WE ARE.

JENIFER M

Express yourself.

OCTOBER 31

Living the Promises

november

"We will suddenly realize that God is doing for us what we could not do for ourselves."

NOVEMBER 1

It was sudden all right. I was hiking a mountain trail about 18 months into my sobriety, alone with my thoughts, and, without warning, was hit by a compulsion to drink so strong that it literally took my breath away.

I sat down, hard, and cried my eyes out from fear and the absolute certainty that all the ego and intellect I had brought to my program to that point wasn't going to be enough to keep me sober in the long run.

And with every fiber of my being, at that moment, I dropped all pretense and opened myself completely to the grace of the God of my understanding and asked for the compulsion to drink and use to be removed, as I vowed to do the footwork.

From that moment on, that compulsion has been removed, from above, just as I asked, while I have done the footwork on earth as promised. **THERE HAS BEEN NO GREATER MOMENT OF TRUTH IN MY LIFE, NO GREATER FOUNDATION ON WHICH TO BUILD THE REST OF THIS BEAUTIFUL LIFE.**

NOVEMBER 2

Trade obsession for good intention.

Here's a quick guide for how to tell the difference between the two:

Obsession is bent on getting its way; intention is interested in finding the best way.

Obsession is self-serving; intention is for the good of all.

Obsession wears you down; intention builds you up.

Obsession is determined to control; intention is committed to influence.

OBSESSION IS FEARFUL; INTENTION IS FAITHFUL.

NOVEMBER 3

"Sad," "lonely," or "angry" are words that describe my mood in any given moment; not a sentence for life.

That's why I try to express feelings as feelings, not as identity.

"I feel sad" speaks to how I am in the moment, whereas "I am sad" sounds as though sadness has taken over my entire being.

It is important to acknowledge my feelings. At the same time, I want to watch that they don't dominate my thoughts or dictate how I see myself overall.

THEY ARE NOT "FOREVER FEELINGS," AFTER ALL.

NOVEMBER 4

Get out in front of your success by what you plan, make time for, and act upon.

A good rule of thumb for this is to plan your day the night before.

Take some quiet time each evening to picture how you would like to support your sobriety the next day: which meeting you'll attend; when you'll call your sponsor; and when you'll make time for prayer, meditation, and step work.

Then you can rest easy knowing you've laid out more than one way to stay connected to your solutions.

IT KEEPS YOUR SOBRIETY FROM BEING AN AFTERTHOUGHT.

JENIFER M

NOVEMBER

What does it mean if you're working your program really hard, but something's still not working?

If you're working the steps and not finding relief, it's not that the program doesn't work; you may not have found the best way—yet—for it to work for you.

You may not have gotten completely honest yet, or found the right perspective yet on your sadness and fear, or developed a relationship yet with a higher power that can restore you to sanity.

You may have one foot in the past while you try to step into the future.

You may be looking for loopholes.

You may be making it harder than it has to be.

Be patient.

YOU MAY JUST NEED TIME.

NOVEMBER 6

Gut Lag: the time it takes for my intuition and my intellect to meet up with my heart.

We get these crazy disconnects sometimes between what we think, what we feel, and what we know.

This tends to create a good bit of confusion.

And we probably shouldn't let just one of these three do the talking.

My head will keep me logical, my intuition keeps me grounded, and my heart moves me forward.

So if you're uncertain about which step to take, ask yourself: "What does my head say to do? What does my gut say? What's in my heart?"

Next, determine the best way to bring all those answers together for maximum impact on you and others.

WRITING THIS OUT REALLY HELPS YOU FIND DIRECTION.

JENIFER M

NOVEMBER 7

I'll take a boring day sober over a "fun" day drunk, any day of the week.

The thing is, sobriety has created too much engagement with life for me to be bored.

Still, I have restful days.

I have times I choose to be a little mindless.

But there is no end to what I can be up to today, now that I'm free to go wherever I want, do what I want, and be whomever I want.

IT'S NOT A PARTY 24/7, BUT IT'S NEVER DULL.

NOVEMBER 8

What are the "givens" in your sobriety?

The non-negotiables in my program are pretty simple, to this day:

Meetings

Steps

Sponsorship—being one and having one

Inventory

Amends

Spiritual connection.

(NOT NECESSARILY IN THAT ORDER.)

NOVEMBER 9

Little shifts add up to big change.

A little smile can improve our whole mood.

A simple prayer can bridge the gap between hopelessness and salvation.

A ONE-HOUR MEETING CAN MEAN THE DIFFERENCE BETWEEN LIFE AND DEATH.

NOVEMBER 10

There's a significant difference between "sight" and "clarity."

Sight is the ability to see things; clarity is the ability to see things as they are, not better or worse than they are.

And clarity comes only when I am willing to suspend instant judgment long enough to consider other possibilities and perspectives.

It doesn't help to rush to conclusions.

AND IT NEVER HURTS TO BE CURIOUS.

NOVEMBER 11

No wish to run, no need to hide...

...no one to fear.

Sobriety brings a great equanimity into our lives, a sense of self-confidence and poise that allows us to walk tall, with our head held high, everywhere we go, knowing that we have done, and **CONTINUE TO DO THE WORK THAT IT TAKES TO LIVE A LIFE OF NO REGRET.**

NOVEMBER 12

Be responsible for your judgments.

Remember, if what you have to say could be

irresponsible,

reckless,

thoughtless, or

insensitive,

THEN DON'T SAY ANYTHING AT ALL.

JENIFER M

NOVEMBER 13

Stay in touch with the pervasive wonder that comes from seeing your life evolve into something beautiful and useful.

Seeing is believing.

So look for your beauty, look for your usefulness.

AND ONCE YOU SEE IT, OWN IT AND CELEBRATE IT.

NOVEMBER 14

Don't hold back—love, live, laugh fully.

When I got sober, I was tentative in every respect. I didn't even know how to laugh right. Everything -- my breath, laughter, emotions—were all caught high up in my throat, for a very long time.

Eventually, when I learned to forgive myself, and when I stopped taking myself so seriously, I relaxed a little, and a little more, and then a little more, until, finally, I could breathe deeply.

And then I could laugh, from deep in my gut.

And then I could love, from deep within my heart.

AND THEN I COULD REALLY LIVE.

JENIFER M

NOVEMBER 15

Sponsor: "Inventory isn't the hard part; it is far harder to let go of your character defects and make your life about something bigger than you."

AND FAR MORE BENEFICIAL, FOR ALL.

NOVEMBER 16

"Turning it over" doesn't just mean handing something over to your Higher Power and letting go;

IT ALSO MEANS LOOKING AT THE FLIP SIDE OF THE THING AND CONSIDERING ANOTHER PERSPECTIVE.

JENIFER M

NOVEMBER 17

I was consumed: by fear, anger, compulsion. By the grace of whatever my Higher Power, I am now possessed—of sweetness and sensibility. Of love, compassion, and the desire to be useful.

I don't need to analyze too much how this came to be; today I simply need to **BE PRESENT TO ITS WONDER**.

Living the Promises

NOVEMBER 18

A beautiful gift of the program today:

I get to choose whether or not a person will have a negative effect on me.

I'm not choosing how they will be; I am choosing the affect I allow them to have on me.

IT IS ONLY WHEN I FORGET I HAVE THAT CHOICE THAT I SUFFER.

JENIFER M

NOVEMBER 19

A deeper form of thanks is acknowledgment.

Tell someone specifically how they have helped you, what you have done with the information, and the difference it will make for your future.

IT IS A GREAT GIFT TO THEM AND REINFORCES THE LESSON FOR YOU.

NOVEMBER 20

We don't make amends to feel good or get ourselves off the hook...

...we do it to make things right, because it's the right thing to do.

TO GAIN FORGIVENESS OR RELIEF IN THE PROCESS IS AN ADDED BLESSING.

NOVEMBER 21

> Learning to say "thank you" without downplaying myself in the process taught me to be gracious, which in turn replaced the false humility that had stood in the way of accepting your kindness and support.

Sometimes a compliment is just a person's way of acknowledging something in you that gives them hope.

In that case, you do as much good for them by accepting their praise as they intend by offering it.

It doesn't matter whether you agree with them, simply appreciate the gesture.

YOU MAY EVEN LEARN A FEW GREAT THINGS ABOUT YOURSELF IN THE PROCESS.

NOVEMBER 22

Education and inspiration don't always go hand in hand.

You can learn the steps, traditions, prayers, and promises, but what will it take to be deeply moved by them?

The answer is within you, and always has been.

SIMPLY DECIDE TO BE.

NOVEMBER 23

One of the great gifts from focusing more on our similarities than our differences is that I come to respect everyone, and am intimidated by no one.

To respect someone doesn't necessarily mean that I admire them.

It means that I can remain respectful, regardless of whether I admire them.

IT MEANS THAT I RECOGNIZE AND RELATE TO THEIR HUMANNESS, WITH ALL ITS FRAILTIES, BECAUSE I AM AWARE OF MY OWN.

NOVEMBER 24

When did I become more interested in being happy and useful than in being right?

Fighting for the wrong thing gets us nowhere and is not to be confused with taking a stand.

Fighting for the wrong thing is just wrestling for control.

Once we see through the delusion of control, we can let go and focus on principles before personalities.

The result is a lightness, energy, and enthusiasm that becomes decidedly more favorable than pushing to be right, heard, and agreed with.

IT'S THE DIFFERENCE BETWEEN WINNING AN ARGUMENT AND MAKING A DIFFERENCE.

NOVEMBER 25

We build character not just by having honorable intentions, but through the countless opportunities we take to manifest them.

NOVEMBER 26

I won't let my happiness be tied to how the day turns out. Instead I'll simply be happy that the day turned up.

And I will do my best to move through it gracefully and purposefully.

I'm sure to stumble, maybe even fall.

But if I do, I will pick myself up, dust myself off, get my balance, and move forward.

AND TOMORROW, BY THE GRACE OF GOD, I WILL HOPEFULLY LIVE TO DANCE THROUGH ANOTHER DAY CLEAN AND SOBER.

JENIFER M

NOVEMBER 27

Working the steps doesn't mean I will forever be above reproach, but it does give me an incredible opportunity to move beyond regret.

REMEMBER "PROGRESS, NOT PERFECTION" AS YOU STRIVE TO MANAGE YOUR MIND AND YOUR CONDUCT FOR MAXIMUM BENEFIT.

NOVEMBER 28

Swinging wildly through the full spectrum of human emotions, to every extreme, doesn't prove that I care; it may just demonstrate how easily I am swayed.

It's easy to get caught up in our emotions.

But when we do, we may mistake the moment and what it can teach us.

Rage can teach us tolerance.

Agitation can teach us patience.

Sadness can teach us happiness.

Fear can teach us faith.

JOY CAN TEACH US GRATITUDE.

NOVEMBER 29

The "I am's" of your life will either build you up or tear you down. If you're going to label yourself, pick the ones that serve the greatest good.

We sometimes label ourselves in ways that aren't always helpful, such as "I am a slow learner" or "I am not worthy," as though those statements are the last word on who we are.

Instead, pick labels that fortify you, like "I am happy," "I can learn anything I set my mind to," "I am worthy of grace and opportunity."

SIMPLY BE CONSCIOUS OF WHETHER WHAT YOU'VE SAID ABOUT YOURSELF IS TRULY WHO YOU WANT TO BE.

NOVEMBER 30

Forgive.

JENIFER M

december

"Are these extravagant promises? We think not. They are being fulfilled among us—sometimes quickly, sometimes slowly. They will always materialize if we work for them."

DECEMBER 1

They certainly seemed extravagant, given my distrustful state of mind when I first read them.

At that time, I knew sorrow, fear, shame, and regret; not freedom, happiness, peace or serenity.

But you promised I would have all of these things—and more—if I did the work.

So I promised to do that work to the best of my ability, one day at a time.

And as I held you to your promise, and you held me to mine, these promises came true.

EVERY SINGLE ONE OF THEM.

Living the Promises

DECEMBER 2

The past doesn't equal the future—for better or for worse—unless I insist on it.

Being clean and sober for even just one day is proof that neither our present nor our future has to equal our messed-up, drunken past.

Proof positive, though perhaps fleeting.

Lasting proof, the kind of solid evidence you can count on, comes from putting many of those days together, one after the other, one day at a time.

AND EACH DAY THAT WE SEPARATE OURSELVES FROM THE MOST BITTER PARTS OF OUR FORMER LIFE, EACH DAY THAT WE IMPROVE, WE BUILD AN ENTIRELY NEW IDENTITY, UNTIL OUR PAST, PRESENT, AND FUTURE ALL TELL A CLEAN, SOBER, AND WONDROUS STORY.

JENIFER M

DECEMBER 3

We often say we're fine when we are anything but.

Don't be afraid to tell it like it is; how else will your fellow travelers know to help you?

And if by "fine" you mean F.I.N.E (as in, F*#%ed up, Insecure, Neurotic, and Egotistical), then say so; there's no shame in it, either way.

By honestly expressing my feelings, and working my way through them, **ONE DAY "FINE" MAY ACTUALLY COME TO MEAN FEELINGS INSIDE NICELY EXPRESSED.**

DECEMBER 4

Today's commitment: less judgment; more compassion.

More compassion leads to more forgiveness.

And more forgiveness equals more love.

SHOULD BE A PRETTY GOOD WAY TO MOVE THROUGH THE DAY.

DECEMBER 5

Because you taught me how to start every day with a clear head and a grateful heart, today, anything is possible.

DECEMBER 6

It doesn't matter how you wake up; what matters is your daily awakening.

There are days when we wake with seemingly unshakable dread, worry, fear, or anger, all of which, when fueled with frustration, put us in danger of calling it quits on our sobriety.

Don't treat the emotions with more emotions; treat them with action: with prayer, contemplation, and meditation.

Treat yourself with loving kindness in the meantime.

EVENTUALLY, THE NEGATIVE EMOTIONS WILL PASS, AND AS LONG AS YOU'RE DOING YOUR BEST, JUST FOR TODAY, TO WORK THE STEPS, CONNECT WITH YOUR HIGHER POWER, AND BE OF SERVICE, YOU WILL AWAKEN TO LASTING PEACE.

JENIFER M

You matter.

In more ways than one.

More than you see.

More than you think.

More than you know.

More than ever.

NEED I SAY MORE?

DECEMBER

7

DECEMBER 8

Of all the things to resist in working a 12-Step program, meetings shouldn't be one of them.

Where else do you get celebrated for being a full-fledged, flawed human being, encouraged as much for making the effort as for meeting the goal?

I'm one of those funny people who has never really fought going to meetings.

In the beginning, the whole "90 in 90" thing was more like 180 in 90 because I was too afraid to not go to meetings.

Eventually, I went because I wanted to share in the experience, strength, and hope of the fellowship, not because I couldn't trust myself to be alone.

Whether I feel like I have to or I want to go, why resist anything in this program that can bring me relief?

I'M JUST SAYING.

DECEMBER 9

The pain from doing deep step work is infinitely preferable to the pain from not doing it.

I learned this lesson from doing a pretty superficial pass through the steps the first time around.

Stuff kept coming back to haunt me.

Relationship stuff, financial stuff, life stuff.

So I did the steps again, and went a little deeper the second time through.

My sense of relief increased. A little.

When I finally took as honest and fearless a look at myself as I possibly could, I experienced an equally profound sense of freedom and serenity.

AS PAINFUL AS IT MAY BE TO CLEAR THE WRECKAGE OF OUR PAST, RARELY HAVE I SEEN A PERSON REGRET THE BLESSINGS THAT COME FROM DOING SO.

DECEMBER 10

Our lives in recovery can be very, very complicated. Thankfully, the solutions are very, very simple.

Not only simple, but easy to find: they're all in the Big Book.

How to relieve my alcoholic suffering?

It's in the book.

How to experience the joy of sobriety?

It's in the book.

How to help others in their recovery?

It's in the book.

I don't need to add to it, embellish it, or reword it.

I just need to read it, and do it, read it and do it, read it and do it.

OVER AND OVER, UNTIL IT STICKS.

JENIFER M

DECEMBER 11

Patient, tolerant, and understanding—it's the only way to fly—literally.

And to drive in traffic, go to work, run errands, be with family or friends, work my program, deal with obstacles, and keep my sanity.

MUTTER IT, WHISPER IT, HOLLER IT IF YOU HAVE TO, BUT MAKE "PATIENCE, TOLERANCE, AND UNDERSTANDING" YOUR MANTRA, TODAY AND EVERY DAY.

Living the Promises

DECEMBER 12

I am eternally grateful for the tools in this program that have moved me from being a sideline critic to an active participant in life.

Tools like willingness.

When we are more willing to strategize than to criticize;

more willing to communicate than to pontificate;

more willing to enhance the world than to just find fault;

THEN WE WILL KNOW WHAT IT MEANS TO BE PART OF THE SOLUTION INSTEAD OF THE PROBLEM.

JENIFER M

DECEMBER 13

Rather than attaching my happiness to people, places, and things,

FOR TODAY I WILL SIMPLY BE HAPPY TO BE ANOTHER LITTLE MIRACLE OF LIFE.

DECEMBER 14

Resist any compulsive urges to make important decisions when you're in the midst of massive uncertainty...

...or you'll risk choosing anything, just to feel like you took action.

PATIENCE ISN'T JUST A VIRTUE, IT'S A MAGNIFICENT STRATEGY FOR WAITING OUT THE STORM OF MY EMOTIONS UNTIL I FIND CLEAR THOUGHT AND DIRECTION.

DECEMBER 15

Sponsor: "You've got to walk through the fire. You can't run around it, you can't jump over it, you can't dig under it. You've got to walk through it. And when you do, the confidence and peace that you'll find on the other side will be more amazing than you ever imagined."

This walk of faith was a pretty big leap for me.

But walk I have, through almost every fire I've encountered in my sobriety, and there have been many.

I haven't always done it with grace or good humor, or appreciated my struggles in the moment, but for the most part, ever since my sponsor so lovingly hammered this into me, I have tried my ever-loving best to walk—calmly and patiently—through each trial.

And each time, I have found the peace and confidence that she spoke of.

IT'S NOT ALWAYS A WALK IN THE PARK, BUT IT'S ALWAYS WORTH IT.

DECEMBER 16

When you feel too tired to take another step (or work one, for that matter), pushing on isn't always the answer.

It's just as important to stop right where you are and recharge;

to empty your mind, relax your body, and rest your weary soul.

IT'S ALL PART OF THE JOURNEY.

DECEMBER 17

> To give in to the laziness of self-pity is to deny the vast, God-given resources within us, and without.

Just because you can't clearly see a solution doesn't mean one doesn't exist.

You have to want to see it.

You have to learn to see it.

You have to want it when you see it.

AND THEN YOU SHALL HAVE IT.

DECEMBER 18

Insanity may be repeating the same mistakes, expecting different results, but delusion is being convinced no one will notice.

We know, deep in our hearts, when we're lying to ourselves.

It appears as strident rationalization or justification of things that obviously don't make sense.

And those closest to us recognize it too.

It's a good idea to give them permission to "call it like they see it" when those delusions cloud our judgment.

IT'S KIND OF HARD—AND THANKFULLY, UNNECESSARY—TO BREAK THROUGH OUR DELUSIONS ALONE.

DECEMBER 19

I pray that I not be too smart for my own good or another's.

Or too stubborn to admit my mistakes.

Or too proud to accept anyone's help.

Or too cynical to consider other perspectives.

OR TOO AFRAID TO BELIEVE IN A POWER GREATER THAN MYSELF.

Living the Promises

DECEMBER 20

The day begins, like any other, and knows nothing of my plans. It is neither pulling for me, nor conspiring against me; it is simply available for whatever I choose to make of it.

DECEMBER 21

There's a big difference between having convictions about this program and being self-righteous about it.

We didn't get here because we were more special than anyone else.

We got here through a divine concert of grace, circumstance, and opportunity.

CARRY OUR MESSAGE OF HOPE WITH HUMBLE, GRATEFUL CERTAINTY, WITH NO SPECK OF SMUG SUPERIORITY FOR HAVING EXPERIENCED IT, AND YOU WILL HELP MORE PEOPLE THAN YOU WILL EVER KNOW.

DECEMBER 22

We can run, we can even hide; that doesn't mean we're not still seen.

DECEMBER 23

Stop working so hard to make things easy.

LET THEM BE, AND EVENTUALLY THEY WILL BE.

DECEMBER 24

We get sober and not only get our lives back, we get our whole selves back:

sober minds;

sober bodies;

sober spirits;

NOT TO MENTION THESE CRAZY HAPPY, SOBER FEET ON WHICH TO TRUDGE, WALK, AND DANCE ON THE PATH.

— JENIFER M

DECEMBER 25

No matter what your spiritual beliefs, today is a beautiful day to contemplate and celebrate redemption, transformation, grace, and love.

DECEMBER 26

There is an earnest and sincere beauty to the conscious transmission of wisdom in the rooms of recovery.

Few places in my life have offered this refuge, maybe none so genuinely.

And all over the world, that lineage has thrived on small donations and big love and fellowship.

WHAT A MARVEL.

JENIFER M

DECEMBER 27

When someone questions your motives, take notice, take inventory, and take ownership (if warranted).

By all means, don't dismiss them just because you think they are unduly taking your inventory; **TAKE TIME TO EXAMINE WHETHER THEY'RE ON TRACK.**

DECEMBER 28

If it is in my heart of hearts to first be of service, then "to thine own self be true" will become the most selfless slogan I can adopt.

Then, being true to myself is the same as being true to whatever gifts I have that are helpful to others.

Being true to those gifts means to recognize and appreciate them.

It means cultivating them.

IT MEANS BEING DEVOTED TO USING THEM IN SERVICE TO OTHERS FIRST, SELF SECOND.

DECEMBER 29

Wake up to the practical, creative, logical, loving, humorous, strategic, playful, determined being that you are, and celebrate the role each facet plays in helping you become happy, joyous, free, and of service.

DECEMBER 30

Self-esteem is a give-then-take proposition.

What is self-esteem anyway?

It is faith in oneself, faith in your abilities.

But blind faith is rarely enough
to convince us of our worth.

To see your value, you have to be of value.

There are a multitude of ways to do that.

Be loving, kind, humorous, empathetic,
compassionate, friendly, understanding.

**THOSE QUALITIES ARE WORTH
A MILLION TIMES MORE THAN
WE GIVE THEM CREDIT FOR.**

Embrace Change.

DECEMBER 31